The High Wolds Heritage Group

Villages Book

Exploring Acklam, Fimber, Fridaythorpe, Huggate, Leavening,

Sledmere, Thixendale and Wetwang

On behalf of the High Wolds
Heritage Group —

Lesley Sharpe

Edited by Lesley Sharpe and Pauline Foster

© High Wolds Heritage Group 2011

First published by High Wolds Heritage Publications

The moral rights of the authors have been asserted.

A CIP catalogue record for this book is available from the British Library.

Book and cover design by Clare Brayshaw

ISBN 978-0-9562495-2-4

Produced, printed and bound by:

York Publishing Services Ltd
64 Hallfield Road
Layerthorpe
York
YO31 7ZQ

www.yps-publishing.co.uk

Contents

Foreword – David Neave   vii

Acknowledgements   ix

Introduction – Dr Colin Hayfield   1

Acklam   10

Farming and the Megginsons of Towthorpe – Sue Dale   20

Fimber   30

Trades and Transport – David Sharpe   40

Fridaythorpe   47

Churches – The Right Reverend David Lunn   57

Huggate   70

Chapels – Chris Whitfield   80

Leavening   91

High Wolds Village Schooling – Trevor Smith   102

Sledmere   114

Dialect – Chris Whitfield   125

Thixendale   132

Wetwang   142

Foreword

By David Neave

This a very welcome publication, researched and written by members of the flourishing High Wolds Heritage Group which is doing so much to highlight and interpret the distinctiveness of these delightful Wolds villages, that range from the stone-built freeholder settlements of Acklam and Leavening to the picturesque landowner dominated estate villages of Sledmere and Thixendale. Although much of the visual character and community spirit of these villages has changed little over the last century, many aspects of village life have been transformed as is illustrated here through the illuminating text and impressive selection of evocative photographs of a lost world. So much that has gone is recorded here – the working horses, the neat corn stacks, the mills, over half the village schools and the dialect. It was a world without cars, where adults and children happily stood in the middle of the quiet roads.

One of the greatest changes must have been the provision of piped water to these dry Wolds villages where there were no streams, and wells were few and very deep. The importance of the village ponds is evident from the introductory chapter and numerous photographs. This importance was underlined by the celebrated 'battle' in 1826 when during a drought the inhabitants of Fimber fought off the invaders from Fridaythorpe who had come to take water from their ponds.

In winter after heavy snow, present-day residents still experience the sense of isolation that was the norm for many villagers before the coming of the car. The railway, so important to Victorian England, had a limited impact on the High Wolds where some villages were as much as five miles from a station. This isolation encouraged self-sufficiency and the lists of village tradesmen and craftsmen in the late 19th century, and the photographs of the shops of grocers, tailors, shoemakers and blacksmiths illustrate this well.

Social life revolved around the church and chapel, particularly the latter, well into the 20th century when despite population decline there was a growth in village organisations, here represented by the WIs and the cricket, football and tennis clubs, their members often named in the captions. It is such information only accessed through oral history that makes this publication, produced by local people with an intimate knowledge of their communities, so valuable.

Acknowledgements

This publication is the culmination of a four-year project supported by the Heritage Lottery Fund.

The High Wolds Heritage Group aims to collect, conserve and make available to the wider community the heritage of the High Wolds villages through exhibitions, publications, talks and visits.

The content of this book represents only a small fraction of the amount of materials collected by members of the HWHG, who will continue their conservation of the heritage of the area beyond this project.

Thank you to all the people in the village communities who have contributed photographs and information for each chapter of this book and to all the authors.

Front cover – Frendal Dale by Kate Fisher www.katefisher-photography.co.uk

Back cover – Thixendale with Worm Dale and Bradeham Dale known locally as Broadholme Dale by Hilary Burton

If anyone has additional information or photographs please contact the following village representatives or www.highwolds.org.uk

Acklam – Keith Holtby
Fimber – Sue Dale
Fridaythorpe – Hazel Acey
Huggate – Sue Dale
Leavening – Sian Langton
Sledmere – Pat Robson
Thixendale – Lesley Sharpe
Wetwang – Sue Ward

Introduction

By Dr Colin Hayfield

Water and the development of settlement and agriculture on the High Wolds

The pattern of settlement and agriculture on the High Wolds of East Yorkshire is not radically different now to how it was in the Victorian period. Villages today are more populous, roads are better and the labour intensive nature of farm work has been heavily diminished. Most of the Victorian houses are still occupied, although the wealth and social status of their occupants has, for the most part, increased dramatically over the last 150 years!

In terms of the human history of the Wolds this would all be regarded as part of the same era no doubt, for our earliest evidence of man's presence on the Wolds goes back some 10,000 years previously to when the first Mesolithic hunters and gatherers crossed the Wolds in pursuit of the animals they hunted.

From the first, it was the natural water sources of the Wolds that determined the location of both the hunted and the hunters; it was those same water sources that determined where man first settled and how they managed the livestock that sustained them. In many cases it is those same water sources that survive today amidst existing settlements; the village ponds, once the carefully managed centres of settlement, but now diminished in size and home to daffodils and ornamental ducks.

This introductory chapter looks more closely at the natural water sources of the Wolds and how they determined the development of the landscape by subsequent generations of Yorkshiremen.

The topography of the Wolds has been shaped by successive periods of glaciation, the soft chalk rock moulded by the ice into broad open wold tops cut by a series of deeply incised dry dales that feed into broader, open, valleys. The chalk rests on impermeable beds of Upper Jurassic clays and creates a water

table at that point. Along the wold scarp that spring line feeds an array of small springs that in turn feed the villages below. However, on the Wolds themselves that spring line surfaces in some of the deeper valleys creating natural ponds, such as those at Burdale or Raisthorpe.

Surface water can run intermittently along such valleys, sometimes just below the surface, sometimes above. Only along the great Wold valley does the 'Gypsey Race' run more or less consistently on the surface.

Glaciation has left its mark in other ways, in particular, glacially derived ponds. Many of these were probably formed from sink holes or dolines that got capped with boulder clay with the retreating ice cap. These natural ponds varied in size from those only a few metres in diameter to those of far more substantial size. They offered sources of both water and clays.

It is some of these smaller ponds that now provide some of the earliest evidence for man's activity on the Wolds. Foremost is Vessey Ponds, a linked pair of ponds that survive into the modern landscape just set back from the wold scarp between Birdsall and Thixendale. A substantial scatter of Mesolithic flints have now been recovered from the field surface around these ponds, and additional flint scatters around other nearby hollows allude to further ponds that failed to survive into the modern landscape.

Similar Mesolithic flint scatters have been found at Wharram Le Street at the spring source of the Gypsey Race.

The quantity of flints suggests that these were 'frequently visited places' for what were essentially still at least semi-nomadic peoples in early prehistory, perhaps places to encamp or feast.

Evidence for Neolithic and Bronze age settlements 4-6,000 years ago are sparse on the high Wolds. However, burial mounds of this period are far more plentiful, often clustered along boundaries; either existing township boundaries or along the great lengths of linear earthworks that enmesh this part of the Wolds. Many of these barrows were fully or partially excavated in the late 19th century by Victorian antiquarians, of which, for the villages we are looking at here, the Driffield corn-factor, J R Mortimer was by far the most prolific. He noted that many of the round barrows comprised deliberate layers of clay as well as chalk. Work around the Wharram Percy and Thixendale barrows suggests that this clay may have been derived from these dolines, either ones that were already dry or ones where the consequent loss of water was deemed acceptable.

We know a little more about Iron Age and Romano-British settlement of this part of the Wolds. It seems likely that many of our existing village sites were settled at this period, odd pottery sherds of this period are known at Thixendale and Wharram le Street, but there is better evidence at Wharram Percy, Burdale and Raisthorpe, for example, where post-medieval village desertion has allowed greater archaeological intervention. Here the village ponds or springs provided obvious settlement advantages.

However, the late Iron Age and Romano-British landscape was characterised by small farmsteads, visible now only by air photography and archaeological fieldwork. Nevertheless these proved quite enduring features of the landscape, some occupied for almost a thousand years, and yet few were situated near to any obvious natural water source. Alongside such little farmsteads are the traces of small enclosed fields. Such farmers would have faced the same challenges as their Victorian counterparts, how to supply water both to the houses and also to any stock penned within the little enclosures.

Higher status Roman sites show that well digging technology was widely available, although the cost of this must have been prohibitive to many, and anyhow, here on the high Wolds the sheer depth of chalk between the surface and the aquifer would surely have been daunting. Even the post-medieval well diggers sought sites on the valley sides where the depth required was more manageable.

Hints at possible solutions come from the Roman-British farmstead site at Wharram Grange crossroads where several bucket-shaped dumps of clay were discovered in a hollowed part of the site. It is possible that elaborate but effective schemes were in place to trap and hold rain water on these sites. Failing all this, arduous daily trips down to the springlines would have been required for household water.

By the late-Saxon, early-medieval period this dispersed agricultural landscape was swept away and instead all settlement became focussed on a smaller number of nucleated village centres, with considerable evidence that such nucleation was carefully planned and laid out. Evidence of such village planning can be seen in Fimber, Fridaythorpe, Wharram le Street and Thixendale, for example; villages that were usually carefully arranged around the central ponds or springs.

Hand in hand with these new village layouts was the organisation of agriculture into an 'open field' system with land allocated and farmed by selions (ridge and furrow). The parts of each field closest to the settlement (infields) were more intensively manured and more frequently cropped, whereas those parts of the fields furthest away (outfields) were less intensively farmed. These outfields were perhaps cropped for a year or two and then left fallow to naturally re-generate (similar perhaps to modern 'set-aside') and probably grazed by sheep or cattle. Further pasturage was provided by the steeper dale sides. Nowhere here were there immediately obvious water sources except for doline ponds like Vessey Ponds.

So sites such as Vessey Ponds were increasingly precious and surviving documentation starts to build from the 12th century onwards – glimpses are provided of the complex arrangements of 'water rakes' or water rights that defined the ways in which neighbouring farmers could enter another's lands to take advantage of the natural waters. 'Wetwang Rakes' was an area of 120 acres lying two townships away, some 4 miles west of the village of Wetwang, in the parish of Bishop Wilton. Such arrangements are also known to have existed in Fimber/Fridaythorpe.

Vessey Ponds provides stark illustrations of this. The ponds are situated within 'Vessey Pastures' a small estate of a couple of hundred acres, bounded for the most part by bronze age earthworks. The water rights to this small ancient estate were subject to a prolonged boundary dispute between the lords of Birdsall and Thixendale, culminating in the last legal 'trial by combat' in England when, on 12th June 1268, in the Castle Yard York, the champion of Peter de Maulay, Lord of Birdsall was vanquished by the champion of St Mary's Abbey York.

Drinking rights at Vessey Ponds appear again in later 17th century documents, when, in 1694, the lord of Birdsall re-asserted his watering rights over the little estate's new owner, William Vessey of Thixendale. This right was re-iterated in the 18th century, when the new owners of Vessey Pasture, the Greames of Sewerby Hall, acknowledged the lord of Birdsall's right to drive 210 sheep onto Vessey pasture entering 'each morning from 10am from Lady Day to Michaelmas and proceed slowly to a spring [sic] near Raisthorpe Grounds where they remain at liberty to graze to Raisthorpe fence till a man can sole a pair of shoes and then to be driven away slowly and right off Mr Greame's estate'. Even in those days lawyers must have enjoyed a 'field day' arguing over the precise interpretation of such a local agreement.

By the 17th century many settlements were shrinking as their rural populations diminished, some eventually becoming completely abandoned, or at least falling into the hands of a single landholder. In some places, such as Burdale, the entire township became given over to one vast sheep walk of about 900 acres. Great flocks were reared across the grassed-over ridge and furrow of the medieval township. Such vast, unenclosed tracts of land allowed the flocks to roam over wold and dale and to access the great spring fed pond in the valley floor that had been the centre of the old village.

Arrangements in the neighbouring township of Towthorpe were different, here holdings in the township were gradually consolidated over a generation or more until the entire township became vested on one family. A coloured map was produced in 1772 that depicted the fields and enclosures, and it was clear that although a proportion of the township remained in arable cultivation, a great swathe of land across the northern border remained open as an enormous sheep walk.

The family that ended-up holding the whole of Towthorpe, the Taylors, built a large and impressive chalk farmhouse, and clearly lived a lifestyle of minor gentry. It was almost certainly they who had built a great well, on the dale side just below the farm. The upper section of the well is 0.8m diameter and constructed initially of neatly shaped blocks of sandstone and then cut chalk blocks below, and is cut (at an approximation) over 34m through the chalk rock into the aquifer. The Ordnance Survey map depicts a well in a similar position nearby the deserted village of Cowlam, which again was farmed from a single holding.

In places like Fimber and Fridaythorpe village water came from the pond (or mere). The Victorian antiquarian, J R Mortimer, who was raised at Fimber, recalls them straining the pond water through a sheet of muslin in order to filter out the worst of the water lice and other impurities, and reciting an older villager saying that he was still perfectly capable of straining his own through his front teeth as he had always done.

Mortimer also talks of community projects to scour out the ponds at irregular intervals and noting that it revealed evidence of earlier minor clay extractions at its base. The nature of this utter dependency on the village pond was starkly illustrated during the drought of 1826 when during the July, the great mere at Fridaythorpe gave out and villagers attempted to share the water of the neighbouring village of Fimber; a sortie that was met with stout and violent resistance from the inhabitants of Fimber, jealous of their own dwindling supplies! As luck would have it a great rainstorm apparently broke the drought the following day!

Tom Denison with his mother, Jane

Some of the earliest photographs that we have of Thixendale, for example, show cottages with a large wooden water butt at the side of the house designed to catch roof water; this softer water was preferred for washing and cooking. Some of the bigger farmhouses took this preservation of roof water a stage further by having large, brick-built, underwater cisterns constructed, often with a hand-pump above. Examples of these can be found at Vessey Pasture Farmhouse and Wharram Grange, both probably constructed in the early 19th century.

From the second half of the 18th century, improving landlords, like the Sykes of Sledmere, were keen to enclose the open landscape of the Wolds. By using new methods of husbandry they sought to break-up the old grasslands and convert them back into arable cultivation. They built new farmsteads out on the Wolds themselves creating farms of 300-500 acres, sometimes more. These were big enterprises with large numbers of draught horses and lads to take care of them. Wold soils are thin and fragile and needed careful handling if they were to be cropped on a regular basis. Top dressings of lime (usually prepared on the farm itself) or bone meal would be applied. High barns were constructed to intensively rear and deep litter cattle over winter so that in the spring cartloads of manure could be taken and spread over the neighbouring fields. Sheep would be carefully grazed over specific fields; manuring on the hoof, so to speak.

Whether it be cattle corralled in a Wolds high barn, sheep enclosed in a field, or draught horses spending the day cultivating a wold top field, all required water. The answer, and in many ways the decisive key to unlocking the enclosure potential of the high Wolds was dewponds. Artificial ponds built strategically at the corners of a number of fields, or just outside a high barn. Hundreds were constructed from the late 18th century onwards with local 'pondmakers' active into the early 20th century to repair or re-line ponds. A few dewponds still survive, but unchecked weed growth progressively damages their

linings and diminishes their effectiveness and many have now become dry and grassed over.

The earliest recorded pondmaker was a Robert Gardiner of Kilham who had begun his working career as a wellsinker; sadly to end his days in 1798 by tripping and falling into one of his own wells. He is first recorded as working in 1775, and a year later was being employed by Christopher Sykes to build ponds for his home farm in Sledmere. Various detailed 'recipes' exist for making a dewpond but it was a huge and arduous task to excavate the chalk, and occasionally, where practical to the chosen location, they are constructed into the natural slope. Then there are combinations of lime, straw, clay and often, particularly around the perimeter, chalk cobbles. Winter times were favoured for pond building as snow would often be rolled in huge snowballs off the field surfaces and into the ponds; it was important that they be filled as quickly as possible so that the clay linings had no chance to dry out and crack.

As the Victorian period progressed, piped water began to be introduced. At Thixendale the need for clean safe water to be available in each home along the street was met by a well being set into the springline at the head of the village. It was a simple, but time-consuming job for individuals to pump the necessary water and carry it back to their homes. Later a large metal tank was raised high on a platform above the well and once filled, gravity allowed pipework to be created to carry water directly into the houses. Young boys or old men were charged with the daily task of pumping the tank full each day.

The photograph shows Martha Midgley, Kate Boyes and Frank Harben at the pump. The pipe runs from the pump to the metal tank. Meanwhile cattle from the home farm and village smallholdings continued to access the village pond below the springline.

Each one of the villages under consideration here developed in its present location because of available water. However, it was man's developing ingenuity to create additional access to water that effectively enabled the agricultural landscape of the Victorian period, the subject of this present collection of essays, to develop and emerge in a form that is still recognisable today.

Acklam

A 1950s view of the cottage where Bob Wardle lived. Opposite is the old Zion Chapel (Primitive Methodist) which was built in 1821. The shed in front is situated on the site of an old school. Behind the signpost, at the top of 'Scotland', is a notice board.

The rectory house, built in 1866 by the ecclesiastical commissioners, came with 57 acres of glebe which included the Coombs. In 1931, after a decade of being uninhabited, it was sold and renamed Acklam Grange. This photo was taken around 1900.

Looking down Main Street. Date unknown, but possibly from the Edwardian era or even earlier. The school can be seen on the left.

Further down Main Street. The first two cottages have since been made into one. The house on the left was demolished around 1960 with the last occupants being the Marwood family.

Top of 'Scotland'. This row of cottages plus the building opposite and the house beyond are long gone. The start of the path in front of the cottages can still be seen today. This photograph was taken from a postcard posted 30.8.1909.

The boy standing to the left of the gate is not known. Doris Jennings sits on the step of the cottage on the left, Edith Jennings sits with the toy cart, Poppy Passman sits on the ground near the barrel and Grandad Jennings stands on the right. The cottages are on the left of the row in the previous photograph.

Mr Jagger. Possibly George Henry Jagger, who farmed at the lodge. Photo taken around 1900 along Bexes. At the time, a gated road. On the right, next to the road up Wold Hill, is a chalk quarry. This disappeared through landscaping during the 1960s-70s.

Wardle family – 1896. There is Frances Wardle, Blanche Grant, Blanche Wardle, Annie Elizabeth Wardle and William Wardle, who was the licensed victualler at the Half Moon Inn for nearly 40 years until his death in 1924, aged 88.

The sign reads: "William Wardle. Licensed retailer of beer, foreign and British wines, spirits and tobacco."

St John the Baptist Church. A very early photo, judging by the size of the fir and yew trees, possibly early 1880s. Although built in 1867, underpinning was necessary in 1900. In 1911 it was badly damaged by a gale and probably it was then that the top of the west tower was removed. The church was finally demolished in 1972.

Approach from Leavening. This photo was taken before WW1. At the time there were 3 cottages here, though none of them remain today. The last residents of the first cottage were George and Ellen (Nellie) Sellers in the late 1930s.

Upstreet towards Acklam Farm. Prospect Farm House and row of cottages at the turn of the 20th century. The footpath in front has since been transformed into gardens.

Greenbank Cottage. Patricia Holtby and Helen Sadowski at their Grandma Blanche Holtby's house during the mid-1950s. The cottage was demolished around 1969 and replaced with a flat-roofed extension for the adjoining Merton House.

Top of Main Street (date unknown). Very little has changed over the years in this scene, except that in this photograph, on the right, there is a footpath and the wall is in good repair.

Pub Corner. Nether Garth and the Half Moon Inn, circa 1900.

Acklam School. The National School was built in 1852 with a capacity for 60 children. With it came an acre of land. Beyond is the village shop and Post Office, run by the Barker family for over 90 years until 1983. With the death of Mrs Gertie Barker, it never reopened.

Last day of school.

Left to right: Dinah Barker, Shirley Marwood, Sylvia Lawn, Joyce Marwood, Keith Marwood, Mavis Midgley, Eunice Wardle, Cynthia Noble, Jean Noble.

In 1947 the west wall collapsed. The children then attended Leavening School. The old school became the church hall and, in 1960, the village hall.

'Scotland'. A 1930s view towards 'Sleights'. What was sometimes known as the 'Village Pond' or 'Sheep washing pool' is Acklam Beck, dammed before it passes under the road. The lady carrying the bucket is Mrs Elizabeth Midgley, wife of Bill.

Manor Farm. Once a Crown farm, this 1950s photo was taken shortly before it became privately owned. A reservoir that supplied the village's water between 1935 and the late 1970s can be seen in the stackyard, surrounded by a square set of metal railings.

Horslay Farm. Built in 1732 and originally owned by a Mr Horslay, it was bought in 1959 by Alf and Eileen Watson. In 1964 they built a new bungalow and transferred the name. A few years later this old farmhouse was demolished.

A view of 'Scotland'. From a postcard dated 1905, the house shown in the centre is the blacksmith's shop. The Rectory is top left and bottom right is part of a row of houses, only one of which remains today.

Farming and the Megginsons of Towthorpe

By Sue Dale

There has been a settlement at Towthorpe, between Wharram-le-Street and Fimber since at least medieval times. Remains of the deserted village can still be seen in a series of earthworks. The first Megginsons arrived in the mid eighteenth century, around 1758 when John Megginson, his wife Hannah, and

their family moved there from Snainton near Scarborough. It is not known why they moved from Snainton but it was probably to come to a larger farm. This first John Megginson began a 'farming notebook', in which he recorded details about the running of the farm.

Towthorpe was owned by the Lloyd Greame family of Sewerby Hall near Bridlington. They had owned it since about 1699 when John Greame married Mary Taylor, daughter of Thomas Taylor of Towthorpe. The Greame family have had a variety of double-barrelled surnames depending on which family they have married into at any one time. They gained considerable land holdings in various counties along with the names. The last Lloyd Greame died in the 1980s without any direct heir and his property passed to the Cunliffe Lister family, distant relatives. The Cunliffe Listers own estates at Burton Agnes near Bridlington and Swinton near Masham at the foot of the Yorkshire Dales. Finally, in 2000 John Megginson and his family, the present occupants of Towthorpe, managed to buy the farm to safeguard the future of the family connection started nearly 250 years previously.

Towthorpe used to be in the parish of Wharram Percy, another deserted village, but when the church at Wharram Percy closed in 1949 it became part of Fimber parish. There are a number of Megginson family graves in Wharram Percy and Fimber churchyards. John's father, Edward, was a church warden at Fimber for fifty years. His parents went to church nearly every Sunday, in the early years by pony and trap.

There has been a farm at Towthorpe since the fifteenth century at least. The two farms that make up Towthorpe now cover an area of 1693 acres. The single farm was divided into two in approximately 1772 according to a map in the Lloyd Greame papers. George Lloyd Greame and Alicia Maria, his wife, made an agreement with Thomas Farthing and William and Dewsbury Megginson, the tenants in 1874, to increase their rents. The old rents had been £640 for 830 acres and £666 for 863 acres (77p/acre) respectively. It was proposed to increase them by £130 and £134 (6p/acre) respectively, a rise of over 7%. The Farthings later moved to Game Slack between Fimber and Wetwang, then to Langtoft before returning to Westfield at Fimber in the 1930s. The Megginsons continued at Towthorpe with a succession of neighbours coming and going.

The farmhouse, a large pre-enclosure dwelling, is built of dressed chalk stone. Chalk was the most readily available building material on the high wolds until the advent of the railways when heavy goods could be more easily transported. Fimber station is only a short distance from Towthorpe but there is a steep hill between the two. The house was split into two when the farm was divided. An extension was added at this time, two storeys immediately next to the house which was then single storey. The roof of the house was raised to provide large dormitories with a separate staircase down into the kitchen. The female servants had separate first floor accommodation in the new extension, their iron-barred bedroom windows facing into the foldyards. Their staircase came down into the farm servants' dining room adjoining the farm kitchen.

There are a number of outhouses in the single storey range constructed of red brick. These comprised a bakehouse, which John remembers being used for separating milk and butter making which took place on a Tuesday, a coal shed and a paraffin/oil house. John and his twin sister Jane can remember having oil lamps to light the house, followed by gas and finally electricity which came to the farm in the 1950s. The schoolroom, which is in the garden, is also brick built and only a single storey. John's father and uncle were taught here by a tutor. There are also two double privies (toilets) in the far corner of the garden. John isn't quite sure who was allowed to use which! Perhaps those nearest the house would be for the family and possibly female servants while those further away would be for the men.

There are two hind houses at Towthorpe, one for each half of the farm. These were built at the end of the nineteenth century from brick. They each had a large 'living' kitchen where everyone ate at one big table. The table would often be built in situ, because of its size, from plain planks of wood. The building of hind houses represents an important social change mirrored elsewhere on larger Wold farms where the farmers became more gentrified and distanced themselves from their workers by employing a hind and constructing a hind house. Sometimes the hind house adjoins the main house, as at Red House Farm at Wharram le Street for example, but is often separate. At Wharram Percy Farm the whole house was designed to incorporate the farmer and his family, and the farmworkers but it was so designed that the only point of potential contact was a single door downstairs. It is recorded that when Cowlam was a single farm of 2000 acres, up to twenty-five men would be seated at the table at once. The hind, or foreman, as he is more usually known now, was the link between the boss (the farmer) and the men. A hind was needed to organise the growing workforce as more land was put under the plough, thus requiring more men and more horses to do the arable work. Previously much of the farm would have been sheep pasture requiring little labour to tend the flock. Many of the single men lived on the farm with others coming in on a daily basis either regularly or just at busy times such as harvest. Although he had his own house, the hind was expected to have men 'living in' with him and his family. His wife was expected to feed these men and wash their bedding. Their work clothes were washed by their mother if she lived close enough or other women in the local village for a nominal fee. The money would be paid to the washerwoman at the end of the year when the man got his own wages from the farmer. Monday was washday. The copper, a large pot, would be filled with water that had to be carried in or pumped up from a cistern. A fire would be lit underneath to heat the water and then soap would be added. Whites would be washed first while the water was still clean, finishing with rougher garments as the water cooled down and got dirtier. It must have been a difficult job getting things dry in wet weather as there were no man-made drip dry fabrics then. Many houses had a drying rack suspended from the ceiling where clothes could be hung to dry out of the way.

Cooking and baking would be a continuous job and the children would be expected to help from an early age with jobs like peeling the potatoes for dinner. Meals consisted of something like milk with cold meat and fruit pie or cheesecake for breakfast and tea with hot meat pie or boiled meat and dumpling with a small beer for dinner (midday). Food would be dished out according to a strict hierarchy with the most important wagoner or horseman first and the least lad (youngest) last in everything. Hands were supposed to be washed before meals. Only one bowl of water was provided. Again the most senior would get the clean water with the last having to use filthy dregs left by everyone else. Sometimes the young lads new to farming would try and avoid washing because their hands were so painful from exposure to all weathers being cracked or chilblained. Wash day would be very busy and drying clothes in winter must have taken days, although people didn't change their clothes as often as we do now and most people would be in their work clothes all day every day. Best clothes were often just clean work things. Wet work clothes were dried outside in the 'slum', a small room in a building on the farm where there was a fireplace. The men would gather here in the evenings in what little leisure time they had to talk, tell stories, sing or play cards.

Tied farm cottages, designed and built for farm labourers, were sometimes built in a village or at the edge of a village, and sometimes, as at Towthorpe, were quite isolated. The cottages were usually for older, married men, often with a family, who worked for weekly/daily wages as opposed to the live-in lads paid at the end of the year. Two pairs of cottages on the edge of the farm at Towthorpe provided further accommodation for workers with another pair of cottages at the end of the road that leads down to the farm. That makes at least ten households on two large farms with other men coming to work from local villages on a daily basis. There may also have been girls and women coming to help in the farmhouse each day. The number of employees needed would have depended to some extent on the size of the farmer's and the hind's families. The more family labour available, the less paid staff was needed. Towthorpe would have been alive with animals, people and activity all day long. Now there is just one full time man and three family members doing the work at home and on a number of other local farms as contractors.

There are also the remains of a set of wold buildings, known as High Barns, away from the main farmstead. These were used for storing fodder (feed) for livestock in winter and for keeping cattle and pigs. They were built of brick with a pantile roof. Very few wold buildings remain, having either been stripped out by people looking for building materials or just left to quietly rot away as their useful life is over. Occasionally they are converted into houses but are usually in remote locations making it difficult and expensive to get mains water and electricity to them. Some, such as the ones at Raisthorpe, had a small cottage incorporated into them when they were built – essentially as a farm cottage but usually intended for the 'beastman' or shepherd. These High Barns were essentially for the winter stalling of fattening cattle. They have been described as 'manure factories' because their main function was to produce a foldyard full of well-rotted manure that could be carted out onto the high wold fields each spring!

On the farm there was a blacksmith's shop with facilities for shoeing horses and a joiners shop. Harry Whitfield, a blacksmith from Wetwang, would visit the farm every Wednesday to do what work was necessary. The brick foldyard and surrounding range of buildings are no longer needed as the farm has no livestock so have been sold off to a developer with the idea of converting them into living accommodation. All the modern agricultural buildings are constructed with steel frames clad with concrete blocks or panels. Their high roofs and large doors with clear floor spans are much better suited to modern farm equipment than the little low-arched brick buildings of the past.

At one time John's family had 1000 sheep which were folded – a field of swedes would be divided up into sections (folds) and the sheep would be given a new section every day having eaten the swedes in the previous day's area. It would be the shepherd's job to 'set nets' each day to make the fold for the following day. This would be done by knocking net stakes (round posts) into the ground in a line and fixing sheep nets (wire fencing) between them to make an enclosure. When the ground was soft this job wasn't too bad but in hard frosts when the ground was solid a hole would first have to be made with a gavelock (iron bar with a point on the end) before the stake could be knocked in. This was a job that could take the shepherd all day. Being a shepherd was considered a full time job and he would rarely be asked to help with anything else on the farm. Sheep kept in this way were hoggs, young sheep born that spring to be sold at the end of winter for meat.

There were also 450 ewes (female sheep) to lamb. Lambing took place in January and April. Originally lambing was done in an open yard and latterly in a covered yard. The shepherd would have some help at this time of year as sheep can lamb at any time of the day or night so someone needed to be checking them at regular intervals. There was a small building nearby which had a fireplace in where the shepherd could brew tea and have a warm up. John can remember cooking chips in a pan on the open fire and a few locals would gather there to play cards, drink beer and eat the chips! He remembers many happy evenings spent in this way. Clover and ryegrass were grown especially for the sheep along with sixty acres of swedes and soft turnips. Water was drawn from the pond to fill the troughs in the yards.

The sheep would be clipped (have their fleeces removed) in May. The fleeces would be stored in the grainary (granary) and then put into wool sheets (large canvas bags) to be sent off to the woollen mills in the West Riding. In 1767

John Megginson recorded in his pocket book *"cliped 662 owld sheep and 266 lambs"*. In August 1770 he records *"selling 220 stone of wool @ 7/6, £82.10.0"*. It was said the wool cheque would pay the rent on a wold farm, which is certainly not the case these days.

The land work was originally done by oxen pulling rudimentary ploughs and later on horses became the main workforce with their attendant horselads and wagoners.

John can remember twelve horses on the farm at Towthorpe with a pony and trap kept for use by his parents and for the shepherd to take lowances out to men working in the fields. The number of horses gradually dwindled as more mechanisation was introduced. The first tractor was a Standard Ford followed by a Fordson Major. They had to be started with a handle at the front to get the engine going. Then a Massey Ferguson came along with hydraulics.

That was really the start of the 'modern' tractor. Even they look like toys compared to the huge machines seen on the farm today. The photograph shows an early tractor on Bridge Farm, close to Towthorpe.

The family's first car was a Hillman, followed by a Morris and then a Standard Vanguard. John's parents didn't go away from the farm much but may have ventured as far as Malton or Driffield. *'Father would go to the Market as this was the farmers' day out. They would go into the livestock market, Malton on a Tuesday or Driffield on a Thursday,*

then to the pub to meet friends.' Corn would be traded on market days. The farmer would take a sample with him and buyers would offer a price depending on the quality. Corn merchants would also visit the farm. Seeds would also be bought and sold on market days, seed merchants sometimes having small 'shops' in or near the market similar to those in the shambles at Malton. Barley, wheat and oats were the main arable crops with the corn being reaped by horse drawn binder, the bundles (sheaves) tied and stooked in the fields to dry. The stooks would then be led 'home' to be stacked at the wold buildings or in the farmyard. September was considered to be the harvest month with the harvest supper taking place once all was safely gathered in, hopefully before bad weather set in for autumn. It was not unknown for sheaves to be left out in the fields in November on the high wolds when it had been a difficult harvest or the farmer was not very well organised. There was a real art to making the stacks look smart as well as providing a waterproof cover to the contents of the stack. The sheaves would then be 'threshed' (the grain separated from the straw) usually by a travelling threshing set. Extra men, often from neighbouring farms, would be drafted in on these days to help the regular men with the work. Young lads would gather round in the hope of killing rats as they ran out of the stacks when they were dismantled. The grain would be put into sacks weighing up to 2cwt (100kg) each and carried up a flight of steps into the grainary. It was something of a competition to see who could carry the heaviest weight the quickest. No wonder so many farm men had bad backs in later life.

This photograph, taken at Bridge Farm, shows an early static baler being powered by a belt attached to a tractor. Loose straw was fed in at one end and oblong bales tied with wire were produced.

Barley and wheat are still grown on the farm together with vining peas for Birds Eye and oilseed rape. Yields of arable crops have improved gradually over the years with the advent of fertilisers and sprays and more scientific plant breeding.

Enormous changes have taken place in the time since the first John Megginson came to Towthorpe, both in agriculture and the wider world. He would be amazed at the size and the complexity of the machines on the farm now and how little labour is needed to grow the crops. However, I am sure he would be very pleased to know there is still a John Megginson there now and branches of the family are spread throughout the Yorkshire Wolds.

The photograph below, taken at Towthorpe in the early 1930s, shows three generations of Megginsons:

John Megginson's father Edward, his mother Muriel with Michael (oldest brother of John), on her knee and Grandfather John Johnson Megginson.

Harvest time in 1950.

Michael, Brian, Jane and John Megginson with friend Valerie Walker, whose father worked on the farm.

The following photograph shows John Megginson with his display at the first exhibition of the High Wolds Heritage Group in 2008.

FIMBER

Interior Fimber Church circa 1988

John Megginson, John Chapman, Betty Walker, Mark Lucas, Ian Wright, Ken Wright, Sheila Wright, Elizabeth Chapman, Sally Chapman, Rev Pat Scott, Sharon Chapman holding baby Georgina Chapman, Andrew Chapman, Betty Wright, Mary Wright Clara Cooper, Jayne Austin, Alan Warren, Nicole Warren.

Fimber WI on roof of Hull Daily Mail building

Joyce Stark, Emmy Barber, Diane Park, Joan Butterworth, Mary Wright, Diane Thompson, Daisy Horsley, Mary Whitfield, Mrs Pudsey, Mrs Acklam, Mrs Fisher.

Sir Richard and Lady Sykes greeting King George VI and Queen Elizabeth, accompanied by Princess Margaret, at Fimber Station July 6th 1948.

David and Julian Cook under the railway bridge on the road from Fimber to Bridge Farm. The boys were related to John and Mary Farthing of Westfield Farm, Fimber.

Chapel of Ease pre-dating St Mary's Church. Date unknown

Interior of Fimber Primitive Methodist Chapel 1946.

Aerial view of Bridge Farm, 1950, home of the Wright family.

Church Row, the cobbler's shop and the Wesleyan Chapel.

The Farthing Family at Game Slack Farm – 1890s

The home of archaeologist J R Mortimer, Fimber. The house stood on the corner of the road to Burdale and Thixendale which is now the site of 'The Gables'.

Wedding of Frank Cook and Julia Farthing.

Graham Bretherick 'sailing' on Fimber pond, Valley Farm in the background.

Fimber cricket team 1970s

Back row: John Farthing, Alec Dale, Arthur Conner, Charlie Grayson, George Alcock, Eric (Butch) Anderson, George Ward
Front row: Raymond Brown, Ron Ives, Sid Oxtoby, John Foster, John Grayson.

Fimber Tennis Club

Back row: Rayner Bretherick, Micky Walker, Richard Horsley, Michael Megginson, Richard Pudsey, Tot Horsley, Jeff Walker, Peter Horsley, Fred Foster, Syd Walker.
Middle row: Mary Farthing, Margaret Horsley, Betty Duke, Daisy Horsley, John Foster, John Farthing.
Front row: Trevor Walker, Graham Walker, Chris Cawthorne.

Graham and Robert Peacock from Wharram, cousin and uncle of John Megginson, skating on Fimber pond in the 1940s.

Aerial view of Fimber Grange.

Fimber Field farmhouse, on the A166 between Fridaythorpe and Wetwang but in the parish of Fimber.

School photo 1931, The Gables in the background.

Tot Horsley in Fimber top pond collecting water – 1930s.

Villagers at a Fimber WI event.

Trades and Transport

By David Sharpe

Nowadays, the villages of the High Wolds support far fewer trades than in former years. The number of businesses has shrunk, with local shops finding it very difficult to compete with modern patterns of shopping. All the villages have lost their full-time post offices and a number are now served by a part-time outreach service.

In contrast, in the late Victorian times, each village was much more self-sufficient, with a comprehensive range of trades serving the local community. The 1892 Bulmer's trade directory records the following businesses in the High Wolds villages:

Acklam

Post office, joiner and grocer, shoemaker, grocer, two blacksmiths, dressmaker, joiner, flour, meal and pig dealer, victualler.

Fimber

Shoemaker, gardener, grocer, tailor, cornfactor

Fridaythorpe

Post office, two dressmakers, two grocers, shoemaker, grocer and blacksmith, victualler, tailor, joiner.

Huggate

Post office at Richard Sisson's, tailor and draper, victualler, two blacksmiths, joiner and wheelwright, sack contractor, shopkeeper, grocer (Richard Sissons), sexton, shoemaker.

Leavening

Post, money order, saving bank, annuity, etc. office; grocer, two joiners, grocer and beerseller, professional nurse, two butchers, victualler, tailor and grocer, blacksmith, miller.

Sledmere

Post, money order, savings bank, insurance and annuity office; victualler, two tailors, bricklayer, woodman, dressmaker, gardener, blacksmith.

Thixendale

Joiner, blacksmith and grocer, victualler.

Sledmere post office

Wetwang

Post office, four grocers, two blacksmiths, two butchers, tailor, boot and shoemaker, joiner and wheelwright, saddler, bricklayer and grocer, two victuallers, tailor and draper, joiner, tailor, bootmaker and dealer, miller.

The wheels of trade and commerce in the villages were oiled in the 19th century through the services of the horse drawn carrier's cart. The carriers provided an invaluable regular service to the local towns, transporting goods and people, especially on market days. Carriers were also well known for their transport of local gossip.

In the 1800s the carrier from Huggate to Driffield left at 8 am and returned at 8pm. The ten mile journey via Tibthorpe took 4 hours

Blowman, tailor at Wetwang

out and 5 hours back. In the early 1900s the local Huggate carrier would go to Wetwang Station (5 miles) to pick up coal for sale to villagers – he timed the journey so that villagers could hitch a ride and catch trains to Driffield or Malton. Trips were also made to Middleton on the Wolds station (5 miles). Villagers brought parcels to Bank House on Wednesday evening for the Thursday morning cart; it usually started its journey with 2 – 3 passengers and picked up further people from outlying farms en route. There was no cover on the cart but it did have a tarpaulin in case of rain. As the 20th Century progressed the role of the horse was taken over by the combustion engine and carriers purchased motor vehicles to replace their horse drawn carts. The role of the carrier was coming to an end and by the 1930s local carriers had ceased to exist. However, some carriers continued their businesses as local bus services.

The 1892 Bulmer's trade directory records the following scheduled carrier services:

Acklam

George Harrison to Malton Tuesday, Wednesday and Saturday

William Mead to Malton on Tuesday, Wednesday and Saturday

Robert Milburn to York on Saturday

Moses Moody to Malton on Saturday

Fimber

Thomas Rudd to Driffield Thursday and Malton Saturday (and grocer)

Fridaythorpe

William Frear to Driffield on Thursday

William Moody to Driffield on Thursday

Huggate

George Dawson (and grocer) to Cross Hill, Driffield (Thursday) and Oddfellows' Arms Pocklington (Saturday)

Leavening

Robert Carr to Malton, Saturday

William Dunn to York, Saturday

John Milburn to York, Saturday

John Peterkin (and grocer) to Malton on Saturday

Waters Robinson (and gardener) to Malton, Wednesday and Saturday

William Severs to Malton, Tuesday, Friday and Saturday

Wetwang

Thomas Agar to Driffield Monday, Thursday and Saturday

William Oxtoby to Driffield Tuesday, Thursday and Saturday (and grocer)

Charles Serginson to Driffield, Thursday

Jesseman Wiles to Driffield, Thursday

The Malton and Driffield Junction Railway

In 1853, a major transport event took place in the High Wolds, with the opening of the Malton and Driffield Junction Railway. This 20 mile line was proposed as a main route from Hull to the North East but was finally built as a single-track branch line. The line opened with a daily service of three passenger trains each way and a pick-up goods daily from Malton.

Although through traffic between Hull and the North East avoided the line and continued to take the route through York, the new line brought benefits to the High Wolds villages. The prices of fertiliser and coal fell due to a reduction in transport costs and farmers were able to transport their produce and livestock to local markets and further afield. Villagers were provided with access to the market towns of Driffield and Malton, but the convenience provided by local carriers ensured their continuation despite the railway. The quarries at North Grimston, Wharram and Burdale used the railway to transport lime and limestone, with traffic to and from Burdale continuing practically up to the line's final closure.

The remote Burdale station served Thixendale. Sledmere and Fimber had their own joint station and Wetwang also had its own station. Fridaythorpe residents had some distance to travel to either Sledmere and Fimber or Wetwang stations and Huggate was some five miles from Wetwang.

Wetwang station staff

The busiest station for passengers on the line was Wetwang, with ticket sales peaking at 8173 in 1901. Passenger numbers for Sledmere and Fimber peaked at 7656 in 1896. Burdale was only beaten by Garton for the title of least busy station. Passenger figures at Burdale peaked at 4291 in 1898; still a large number considering the remoteness.

The busiest station for freight was Sledmere and Fimber with receipts of £1716 in 1912. Next came Wharram with receipts of £977 in 1912 followed by Wetwang with receipts of £963. In 1912 Burdale received £279 for freight. The major goods arriving at the stations by train were coal, fertiliser and feed, accompanied by small parcels. The coal provided the Station Master with a lucrative sideline as a coal merchant. The produce shipped from the stations were wheat, barley and oats. In addition to these minerals and grain, the transport of livestock played an important part, with Sledmere and Fimber handling 10271 livestock wagons in 1907. Dedicated mineral trains were introduced in the 1920s to transport limestone to Thirsk and then onward to Teeside.

In his book "When horses were supreme" Herbert L Day describes the process of taking produce to the local station by horse-drawn wagon and returning to the farm with commodities such as coal, fertiliser and feed. He describes a trip he made one winter in the 1920s from Broadholme farm, above Thixendale, to Burdale station in order to collect a load of cattle cake. It was late afternoon and fallen snow had been melting during the day. Having loaded up his wagon he set off along the road from Burdale to Thixendale, to find the snow had frozen again in the failing light, making the road treacherous for his team of four horses. Herbert needed to call upon all his experience as a wagoner if he and his horses were to get home safely. He writes:

"There was no alternative. In order to control my team I had to ride my nearside pole horse and drive the leading pair from this position. I rode without my feet in the stirrups, ready to jump clear should the horse lose its footing. Occasionally its hind feet slipped forward under its belly, but the horse carried me safely to Thixendale.

I dare not attempt the hill which was the last lap of my journey, so I stopped at the blacksmith's shop. He removed two nails from each of the horses' shoes and replaced them with stud nails, 32 in all. It was dark, so he worked with the aid of a stable lamp. The horses were now able to pull the wagon with more confidence, and I was relieved of my anxiety. Nevertheless they were lathered with sweat before I arrived at the farm, and no doubt fear had played a part."

This story illustrates the importance of horses in an integrated transport system, which continued until the 1930s, and the skills required of the men hired to manage the horses.

The passenger train service survived two world wars and nationalisation but finally succumbed to the inevitable and closed in June 1950. The

An early horse team at Thixendale

goods service continued with a pick-up goods running on Tuesday and Thursday along the length of the line and to Sledmere on Saturday. Postal services had to be reorganised, with the mail no longer coming by passenger train. With the closure of the last quarry, Burdale, in 1955, the line was doomed. The last goods train ran from Malton to Sledmere and back on Saturday 18th October 1958.

Passenger and Goods traffic figures are from the definitive history of the Malton and Driffield Railway: The Malton & Driffield Junction Railway by Warwick Burton published by Martin Bairstow.

Thanks to Trevor Smith for the material on Huggate carriers.

Fridaythorpe

Riggs Farm, Fridaythorpe in the 1950s. The yard with corn stacks is ready for thrashing day. The photo shows the foldyard enclosed by stables, cowsheds, barns and granaries etc. adjoining the farmhouse. All were built of chalk.

Bottom pond at Fridaythorpe in 1914. On the left Edmonds Farm, Rawlings Cottage and Manor House Farm with the Old Mill in the background.

Winter at Fridaythorpe in the early 1950s. Bottom right is Manor House farm when part of the farmhouse was turned into a cafe. The Methodist Chapel is also on the right and there are two ponds. Top left near the trees is the Reading Room where mainly the men went to play snooker, billiards, cards, dominoes, etc.

There were two ponds at Fridaythorpe until the early 1970s when the Top Pond was filled in. There was a footpath which ran at the back of the Top pond and between it and the Bottom Pond with a small bridge in the centre so when the Top pond was above a certain level it flowed into the Bottom pond. On the right is the chalk track where cattle and horses came down to drink.

Fridaythorpe AFC 1948.

L to R: Claude Lakes, Bill Boyes, Cyril Walker, Harry Lawson, Jack Wharram, Fred Pickering, Ken Hotham, Jeff Walker, Len Sowersby, George Rawlings, Bob Acklam, David Yates, Ernest Walker and Harry Milner.

This was Fridaythorpe cricket team in 1937 when they won the Wolds Cup.

Back row Will Redhead, Johnny Boyes, Alf Bretherick, Eddie Sowersby, Cyril Lakes, George Rawlings. Front row Cyril Walker, Cecil Boyes, Rayner Bretherick, Ossie Brent and Tommy Rawlings.

Back Street, Fridaythorpe in 1956. The cottage on the right was home to George and Nellie Rawlings and their mother. To the left was Edmonds Farm, where Les Pexton and his family farmed, and the Methodist Chapel that was demolished in the early 1990s.

The Old Corn Mill at Fridaythorpe as it was in 1918. It stood in the field to the west of where Wold View is now. The grass track leading to where the Mill was can still be seen.

Harvesting at Fridaythorpe in the 1940s with Clarice Boyes astride one of the horses to control them as they pull the binder, cutting and tying the sheaves of corn ready to be stooked.

Gathering in the harvest near Fridaythorpe in 1958 are Olive and Pearl Milner, forking the sheaves to Ted Hall to load onto the trailer that has gormers at each end of it to hold the sheaves in place. Harry Milner stands near the tractor waiting to transport them to the stackyard.

Looking across the Top pond towards Mere Farm in 1922. The two cottages that stood next to the footpath between the two ponds in the distance to the left are four chalk cottages that were behind the Bottom pond.

The ornately carved reredos and altar at St Mary & St James' Church, Fridaythorpe. The altar rail is Jacobean from c.1620 and the Bishop's chair to the left of the altar was made by the village joiner from the original oak roof in 1902.

The date is unknown when St. Mary and St. James' Church was built at Fridaythorpe; parts of it date back to Norman times. Within the south porch the arch of the doorway is richly decorated as is the Chancel arch; the font is plain but all are Norman. Outside on the west tower is an unusual clock which has a black and white painted oak face and an inscription which reads "Time is short, eternity is long". – 1903.

Blacksmiths Shop Fridaythorpe

Fridaythorpe blacksmith's house and next to it is the smithy with a trailer typical of the early 1900s. The cottage on the right was known as "Granny Ripley's".

Main Street, Fridaythorpe early 1920s. On the right is Rose and Crown farm which, in the late 1800s, was also the village pub. On the opposite side of the street is the Primitive Methodist Chapel 1851. The girl standing near the wall of Holme Farm is Madge Lyus, née Boyes, whose father was the landlord of the Rose and Crown pub, which by then was in the white house halfway up the street on the right.

Preceded by two tractors, this threshing machine makes its way near Pefham Wood on the York road in February 1947. The two men walking are Harry Lawson on the left and Billy Wilson. On the tractors were Bill Coupland senior and Will Redhead who owned the threshing set.

Main Street Fridaythorpe February 1947. The threshing machine and tractors make their way towards York. On the left is Acklam's village shop and on the right Mill Farm.

Albert Bassett, the village blacksmith, outside the smithy in 1926. On the wall is a poster advertising Driffield Show. The anvil and forge with the bellows were on the left and horses were shod in the building on the right. Villagers of all ages would call in to see what was being made or whose horse was being shod, but mainly in winter for a warm near the fire.

Fridaythorpe School was erected in 1902 and closed in 1983-4. The school prior to this was situated on Back Street where the Beacon now stands. Children aged 11 years upwards from Thixendale, Fimber and Burdale also attended the school from around the late 1940s. Eventually, when their village schools closed, all the children came to Fridaythorpe. In 1956 children aged 11 and over were educated at Driffield County Secondary School.

The senior children of Fridaythorpe School on their annual educational outing to York in 1953.

Back row: Joyce Stark, Doreen Morley, Ivy Jefferson, Emma Barber, Edna Pickering, Norah Grantham, Pearl Milner, Jessie Barber.
Middle row: Tony Birdsall, John Walker, ??, Des Ward, Brian Hill, Charles Ward.
Front row: Terry Duggleby, Keith Wilmot, Lester Bell, Norman Coupland, Harry Boyes, Ken Wilson.

Churches

By The Right Reverend David Lunn

By Way of Introduction

The High Wolds Heritage Group has a remit to care for the past, present and future of five and a half ancient parishes. And within these five and a half parishes are eight churches – not all ancient. The roll call goes like this: Acklam with Leavening, Fridaythorpe, Huggate, Sledmere, Wetwang with Fimber, and half of Wharram Percy, which for us means Thixendale. They all have a strongly individual history, mostly with their own vicar (a rector at Huggate), living in his vicarage (a rectory at Huggate), at least in theory, in the middle of his flock. Though all, except Huggate, were in the rural deanery of Buckrose, those never very strong links would be seriously weakened by the fact that Acklam, Fridaythorpe and Wetwang were all 'peculiars' whose links with York Minster brought them within the 'Liberty of St Peter' – a sort of state within the state. Similarly there were links between Sledmere and Kirkham Abbey (through Sledmere's mother parish of Kirkby Grindalythe) and Wharram Percy and Haltemprice Priory. These ancient, and largely forgotten links, had one disastrous consequence: the income from tithes that was meant to support the ministry of the local church was irrevocably diverted away from the parish and this left the vicars of these churches, for the most part, with a pitiful income. Sledmere was the worst off. Archbishop Sharp in about 1700 lamented that "the impropriation is now in the hands of Mr Rogers of Escrick and another; they allow but £8 per annum for the service of it, so that it is with much difficulty that a curate is got, at the present Mr Leech comes now and then, but is weary of it." Only in the second half of the 19th century was a serious attempt made to ensure that there was a vicar in each parish with a decent house and an adequate stipend. The following century, 1865 to 1965, was perhaps the golden age of the Church of England. But, alas, the last fifty years have seen the dramatic collapse of this, perhaps over confident, experiment with a constant reshuffling of the parishes into varying combinations. Today

Acklam and Leavening, with Birdsall, Burythorpe, Langton, North Grimston, Settrington and Westow are all within the united and happily named parish of West Buckrose. Huggate is one of the nine parishes that comprise the united benefices of Pocklington Wold and Londesbrough Wold. The others are Burnby, Hayton, Londesbrough, Shiptonthorpe, Great Givendale, Millington, Nunburnholme and Pocklington. With greater simplicity, just for the moment Fimber, Fridaythorpe, Sledmere, Thixendale and Wetwang, with tiny Cowlam, work happily together in the interestingly named Waggoners benefice but plots are afoot to link the Waggoners to their neighbouring six-parish Woldsburn benefice. Perhaps, optimistically we can see the High Wolds parishes as the beating heart of this vast conglomeration! It is certainly all a bit messy and proper vicars living in proper vicarages are now scarcer than hen's teeth. Is this really going to be the face of the future?

The Building History of nearly all our High Wolds Churches, and indeed of most of the churches of our neighbourhood can be focussed into two half centuries: 1110 –1160 and 1860 – 1910.

The Twelfth century brought some boom years to Yorkshire. The new king, Henry I (1100 – 1135) brought in a new wave of Norman landowners, "men possibly less fastidious than William the Conqueror's followers and more willing to eat the oaten bread of these northern lands." They soon turned into home-bred Yorkshiremen and invested their wealth in the great new monasteries — Kirkham, Rievaulx, Fountains, St Mary's York, and many many others. And they built churches— 'they came up', it was said at the time, 'like mushrooms in the night'. The archbishop also prospered. In 1065 his lands had been worth annually £320. By 1086, thanks to William's brutal peace keeping, that had shrunk to £166. But less than a century later, in 1180, he was receiving £1180. All our High Wolds churches were linked to a greater or lesser extent either to York Minster or to the new local monasteries. Though in the long run these links were to prove very harmful, way back in the 12th century they gave the leadership and the capital needed to bring back to fertility and so prosperity a derelict landscape. And these new, (or perhaps restored) communities needed a church and a burial ground to mark their place in both the temporal and supernatural framework of their 12th century world. And for the Normans that 'House of God' had to be in stone. We can only speculate why the Anglo-Saxons spurned the stone debris left by their Roman predecessors and built all their halls and most of their churches in wood. But we can be grateful that the Normans loved stone. Excavations at the ruined church of Wharram Percy showed that a 10th century wooden church occupied the same site as the later stone building. It is probable that the 12th century churches at Huggate, Fridaythorpe and Wetwang were built in already ancient burial grounds whose wooden churches had perished in the 'harrying of the North' fifty years earlier. But the Norman determination that their churches were to be built of good stone, and not just the rubbishy chalk that was under their feet, was making statements both about the future, 'We are here to stay', and the past, 'we are bringing back the ancient glories of Rome'. And the significant amount of stone reclaimed from the derelict remains of centuries – old Roman villas to be found in these ancient churches, supports the view of the modern experts that these Norman church builders chose this material, not simply because it was the cheapest option but because it was Roman.

These three surviving 12th century churches were not large. Wharram-le-Street, just next door, gives us a good idea of what they looked like. Standing in the main part of the nave of Wetwang church with the original south wall largely intact you can get some feel of that first stone church. In the first hundred years of its life it was extended three times, first the north aisle, then an extra bay to the nave and lastly, in about 1260 say the experts, came the large Lady Chapel.

Meanwhile they had built a tower, which rather oddly, and exactly like that at Wharram Percy, cuts into the newly built west bay of the nave. As you look about you, all these additions and joinings on can be clearly seen. To the east when the church was first built (say 1130?) the chancel would be a small semi-circular apse but these went out of fashion in the later middle ages and at

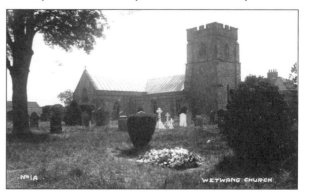

some point this would be replaced by what now seems like a traditional east end with a window above the High Altar. An inscription over the south door of nearby Weaverthorpe Church makes it certain that it was built in about 1120. The Revd E. Maule Cole, Wetwang's immensely learned 19th century vicar, assures us that Wetwang church was built in the time of archbishop Thurstan who died in 1140. Fridaythorpe and Wetwang, for both belonged to the Wetwang Prebend, may well have been built more or less simultaneously. Very oddly, on one of the Norman pillars at Fridaythorpe is the cryptic inscription *"This 713 found hear"*. The English wording alone makes it clear that this cannot go back to 713 A.D.! It must be an ancient bit of graffiti that once meant something profound to someone.

Huggate's very beautiful, and in this part of the world unusual, tower and spire disguises the fact that this too is in essence yet another building that hasn't really changed since it was built in this same astonishing first half of the 12th century. And in each of these churches can still be seen, and still in use, a huge font. These go back to the very beginning of church life in these villages and could be older than the churches themselves, you can have a wooden church but you can't have a wooden font. These huge stone fonts were clearly very important to the Norman church builders in this neighbourhood. Sometimes they are elaborately carved as at Cowlam, Cottam (now in Langtoft church), Bainton and Kirkburn but even when as in these three churches they are comparatively plain, they are noble and awe-inspiring works of art.

Astonishingly these three churches have survived sufficiently unchanged to be easily recognizable by visiting ghosts from the past. But others have perished. At Sledmere the mediaeval tower is a survivor of a building, much the same size as the present modern church that was so dilapidated by the 18th century that it was replaced by a small Georgian building that was to be swept away in its turn in the 19th century. Acklam is a mystery. The village lies just down from the Wolds on the jurassic limestone from which its houses are built. But in 1864 the curate there tells the Archbishop that the church is "one *of the most comfortless and dilapidated places in His Grace's diocese*". All trace of that building vanished four years later with the building of a very large new church which in its turn was to be demolished a century later leaving only a pleasant open space, with a seat, in the middle of a wonderful wild-life churchyard.

Fimber has its mysteries too. When 'the small ancient building in the midst of a fruitful garden' was demolished to make room for its 1871 replacement, there were revealed not only what might have been an Anglo-Saxon pagan temple, but also the foundations 'of a church much larger and  apparently more ancient than the "little edifice" that had just been demolished.' And in the scattered parish of Wharram Percy from 1325 there was certainly 'The Chapell of Saynt Katheryn in the town of Tothorpe' and probably a chapel at Thixendale and possibly one at Raisthorpe. At Thixendale we are told that in about 1920 'a few of the old people insisted that in the far-distant past, the Township had had a little Church or Chapel. They were fond of pointing out the traditional spot about a mile from the village'. The 1443 settlement of the Vicar's stipend makes it clear that this is meant to cover too the cost of a 'chaplain for to celebrate in the towns of Sixendale and Raisthorpe'. And there is evidence as late as 1541 that services were taking place at Thixendale, Raisthorpe and possibly Burdale. But the Towthorpe Chapel was certainly closed in 1547 under the iniquitous Chantries Act and the chaplain's modest income of £4 12s 4d confiscated by the Government of the day. We know his name, Robert Baynton, and my guess is that he took services at Thixendale and Raisthorpe as well and that, when he went, those services ceased and the people of these outlying communities had to get used to the long trek over the hill to their parish church at Wharram Percy.

Fortunately, after the excitements of the 12th century, we can cover the next seven hundred years in two sentences. The Normans built well and their churches, if 'the head and the feet are kept dry', will last for ever. There would be changes, bigger windows in the 15th century and bigger pulpits and less colour in the 16th, but almost all the evidence of what was done in these long centuries was to be swept away in that extraordinary upsurge of building and restoring that must have almost overwhelmed our villages in the half century between 1860 and 1910.

The 19th century: New Churches, Vicarages and Schools

The unique Religious Census of 1851 shocked the Church of England with its revelation that the Wesleyan and Primitive Methodist Chapels had many more adherents in many villages than the Parish Church. It was noticed too that this was particularly true in those villages in which for centuries there had been no resident parson. The determination became strong that there must be a church, a vicarage and a church school in every village. 18th century enclosures had strengthened the finances of both the landowners and the clergy. The 1840 reforms of the Church of England, which had released much of the wealth of the Cathedrals for the benefit of the wider church and also greatly simplified the procedures for creating and endowing new parishes, had the unexpected result of a very fruitful relationship with local benefactors. Then for us here in York Diocese the appointment, as surprising to him as to everyone else, in 1862 of William Thomson as archbishop, brought to this sleepy outpost of the Church of England an efficient (though not necessarily likeable) leader who was determined that there should be a vicarage and a school in every parish and that the abuses of pluralism and non-residence should cease.

The shock of change came first to Huggate. James, Lord de Saumarez, had become rector in 1825 and he seems never to have visited the parish! But he did give them a handsome set of silver. The parish was looked after by the resident curate, Thomas Rankin who, rather obligingly, died at the age of 80, certainly unlamented by the new Rector, Edward Curtis, who lamented that '*dissent had been taught and practised by the curate in sole charge for 42 years.*' And the new Rector moved with astonishing speed. The new very splendid rectory was up within a year, (still there, now Kirkdale House), and barely a year later he was able to report to the new archbishop that there had been '*a complete restoration of the fabric. North and South aisles and chancel rebuilt. The whole reseated and a new roof.*' Alas, he meant well and I wonder who paid?

From outside, Huggate church is beautiful but within, one could wish that the 1864 woodwork was elsewhere.

Acklam was nearly as quick off the mark. Thomas Browne had become vicar in 1864 but in 1865 he was still looking after his former parish of Hilston and acting as curate of Roos. He might have been waiting until the new house was ready for him in 1866, when it and the living changed from a vicarage to a rectory. But the decision to replace the old '*gloomy and dilapidated*' church must have been taken quickly for the new church was ready for use by 1868. J.B. & W. Atkinson was a York firm of architects with a big local practice. This church, built in a churchyard well away from the village, was itself demolished in 1972. Nearby Burythorpe church, also well away from its village, was by the same architect and though smaller, gives us some idea of what St. John the Baptist, Acklam must have looked like.

Meanwhile two more grand new vicarages were being built at Fridaythorpe and Wetwang. That even now, after nearly a century and a half and surrounded by trees, they hardly fit into their village landscape, highlights the architectural impact of the national railway network. The Ecclesiastical Commissioners rather reluctantly had accepted a special responsibility to help those parishes that were linked to those abolished cathedral prebends which were the source of their wealth. So these two new vicarages would be being built at the request of the archbishop with joint funding from the local landowner, Sir Tatton Sykes, and the Ecclesiastical Commissioners and with the Commissioners' money came the Commissioners' architect, Ewan Christian. In fact they are not as grand as they look. They were thoughtfully designed to give a home for a man and a family of moderate wealth — the vicars of Fridaythorpe and Wetwang would each have a stipend of about £200 a year — who would be expected out of that to pay for a live-in maid and possibly a man to help with the horse and the garden. The Victorians were surprisingly realistic about class.

If the vicar was to exert a proper influence on the *'better sort of people'* he had a *'position to maintain'* and the right house was important in that. In this decade six new vicarages were built in these six parishes. None are now owned by the church, but all are still lived in and very much in use. That 'The Old Vicarage' is the most sought after address for the aspiring middle classes and that these houses do still make a splendid family home shows that these Victorian vicarage architects were not without wisdom.

For completeness I should add that (a) Sledmere's new vicarage was in part an adaptation of an existing 18th century house, (b) there were plans made for a vicarage at Fimber but it was never built, and (c) the old vicarage at Wetwang is currently offered for sale at £845,000.

These Wetwang and Fridaythorpe vicarages have introduced the Sykes family into our narrative. By the beginning of the 19th century they had come to own all of Sledmere, nearly all of Fimber, most of Wetwang and Thixendale and much of Fridaythorpe, together with vast acreages in the surrounding neighbourhood. For nearly a century, from 1823 until 1913, two Sir Tatton Sykes, father and son, ruled this vast empire. Sir Tatton I, who died in 1863, had set the pattern of a practical concern not only for the agricultural well-being of his estates but for the infrastructure of the villages. Influenced by his wife, Mary Ann, Lady Sykes, their first concern was with education. At her funeral the coffin was *'preceded by a choir made up of the schoolmasters from her village schools'*. There is a fine memorial window to her in Wetwang Church and, more tellingly, Wetwang School, built in 1843, as the inscription still tells us, is said to be the oldest village school in the East Riding still in use. Sir Tatton I, too, set the pattern of using the best architect available. J L Pearson, later to be the architect of Truro Cathedral, was the chosen architect for the restoration of Bishop Wilton, Kirkburn and Garton between 1856 and 1859. Though Sir Tatton I had died before the Wetwang and Fridaythorpe vicarages were completed it must have been at his instigation that they were built. His son and heir, Sir Tatton Sykes II, was about as different from his father as two people can be, but like his father he wanted to see churches, vicarages and schools in the villages of his estates and like his father he believed in using only the best architects. But for Sir Tatton II church building was something of an obsession. He built seven new churches and restored, sometimes almost a new-build, eight others. On his death bed in London in 1913, almost his last words were 'I must get back to Sledmere and build some more churches.' At first the new baronet continued to work with his father's architect of choice J L Pearson and he was asked to prepare plans for the new churches at Thixendale and Wansford. But there was a falling out and in the decade 1867—77 it was G E Street who designed seven new churches (and built six; Duggleby never got off the drawing board) and restored five others. Then there came a further falling out and a pause in the church building campaign until, in the 1890s, the great work started again with a new generation of architects.

In Thixendale we see most dramatically what Sir Tatton II was striving to achieve: a village community with, at its heart, a school, a vicarage with a resident vicar and a church all designed by an architect of the highest ability and in a style designed to uplift the hearts and minds of those who used them from the mundane to the eternal. Thixendale was fortunate in its first vicar. The Revd W H Fox came to the new vicarage and church in 1870 and remained there until his death in 1911. His 'Annals', which miraculously have survived, give a moving picture of the life of the church and village throughout these 40 years. The earliest place of worship in modern times was the Wesleyan Chapel built in 1837. A Schoolroom was built in 1849 and in 1854 this was licensed for worship. The Communion Silver still in regular use at Thixendale is inscribed 'The gift of Lady Sykes to Thixendale Church 1855'. In the building of Thixendale Church and the creation of the new parish there is an intriguing meeting together of the old ways and the new in the 19th century church. Thixendale was still within the ancient parish of Wharram Percy. There the vicar from 1832 until 1877 was Robert Ellis. He was also Vicar of Wharram-le-Street, (1832—1877) Vicar of Acaster Malbis (1829—1868) and Vicar of Birdsall from 1831 until his death in 1880 at the age of 90. He had a curate living at Birdsall where 'he gave some slight help two or three times a year' and at Acaster Malbis where, we are told in 1864, 'he has not officiated for years.' None of this made much sense. None of these were 'rich livings.' He lived in some style at North Grimston and was Justice of the Peace for the East Riding. But his total ecclesiastical income was £285 from which he would have to pay at least £50 each to his curates. He must have acquiesced in the changes at Thixendale for without his approval nothing could have been done.

The new church at Fimber was being built more or less simultaneously as that at Thixendale. It illustrates the truth that each of G E Street's churches is a unique masterpiece designed both to complement the geography and the pastoral needs of this particular place. We can be fairly certain that Ewan Christian sent out his plans for the Wetwang and Fridaythorpe vicarages without ever having set foot in those villages. At first sight we would not think that Fimber was designed by the same architect as Thixendale. It is much smaller, it is built of stone not brick and there is no provision for a robed choir. But then Fimber was a 'chapel of ease' and not a parish church. And unlike Thixendale, which crouches with its neighbours in the security of its hidden valley, Fimber, or at least Fimber church, is '*a city set on a hill that must not be hid*' with a steeple that is the centre point of the view as you approach from Wetwang and Sledmere. And though it is a modest building appropriate to a small village there is nothing mean or cut-price about it. This is shown by the noble lychgate of solid stone, which Pevsner, accurately I suppose, calls an archway. And in Fimber, as in Thixendale and every 'Sykes' church, there is magnificent stained glass in every window, including those in the vestry. We have come to understand that the best Victorian stained glass is at least as good as any that has ever been made. And to see such glass at its best you cannot do better than to visit the four High Wolds 'Sykes' churches at Thixendale, Fimber, Sledmere and Wetwang.

By 1880 the church builders' hammers had fallen silent. There are two obvious explanations. The first is simply that the main aim of the Anglican revival of the 1860s, a church vicarage and school in every parish, had, rather astonishingly, been achieved in fifteen years and there was nothing left to build! The more usual explanation is that the farming crisis brought about by the massive imports of wheat from America meant that the local landowners could no longer afford the luxury of building churches. These are probably both true, but come the 1890s, they did not stop Sir Tatton Sykes from finding both the churches that needed building or restoring and the vast sums needed to carry out these ambitious schemes. A possible explanation for Sir Tatton Sykes improbable years of restraint is that he was deeply involved in the eventually abortive scheme to build a vast Roman Catholic Gothic Cathedral in the heart of London. Sir Tatton Sykes' wife, who had converted to Roman Catholicism, was convinced she could persuade her husband to finance the project. I think he was tempted by the prospect of being involved in the building of a second Westminster Abbey. It was on the rebound that, with his new favourite architect Temple Moore, he set about building, with no expense spared, the best parish church in the world. Inevitably this was to be at Sledmere where the Georgian box built by his great grandfather within the mediaeval church, despite the steady enrichment of its furnishings, was not what the 5th baronet thought a church should be like. In 1893 it was swept away, (fortunately pictures of it survive in today's church) and in the next five years the new St Mary's church at Sledmere emerged. What makes it extraordinary is the sheer quality of the workmanship in every part of the building — woodwork and stonework all carved by experts, great statues, wonderful windows. It is not liked by everyone, *'quite perfect and patently dull'* says one critic but it has also been called *'one of the loveliest churches of England'*. It is all exciting ('dull'? The man must be mad!) but you come close to perfection in the proportions and decoration of the chancel which, as in a cathedral or monastic church, works splendidly as a separate church. It has its faults: despite the £60,000 or more it cost (£millions in today's money) it has a heating system that at its best only reminds you how bitterly cold you are; and, oh that it had been built somewhere with a growing population that needed a new church or at least in the *middle* of Sledmere.

Good relations between Sir Tatton II and his architect Temple Moore did not survive the building of Sledmere church and, when in 'A.D. 1900 Sir Tatton Sykes determined to restore Wetwang Church, the work was entrusted to Mr Hodgson Fowler of Durham'. He is the least well known of Sir Tatton Sykes' quartet of architects but Wetwang has good reason to be grateful for the choice. The Revd E Maule Cole tells us that *'having been President of the East Riding Antiquarian Society, he felt that he ought to set an example of a perfectly restored church and refused to allow any removal of what was really old. To this Mr Fowler readily consented... and so the present church is a model of church restoration.'* And indeed it is! The chancel, the roof, the pews, and all but one of the stained glass windows were new in 1901 or soon after and yet the building still has the calm and sense of unity of an ancient parish church. Curiously the restoration of Fridaythorpe, carried out by the same architect at much the same time as that of Wetwang, is a good deal less successful. Both the aisle and the porch that were rebuilt in 1901 have needed to be rebuilt again in the 21st century and a small church is made to feel smaller by the screening off of the Chancel and the replacement of the East Window by an overlarge reredos brought from the demolished church at Sledmere. Uniquely there hang on the walls a series of paintings of the church as it was before its restoration. These give us a wonderful insight into what all our churches must have been like before the good intentions and deep pockets of the restorers took them in hand.

The Twentieth Century

Three funerals, two in 1911 and one in 1913, marked the beginning of the 20th century for the church in this neighbourhood. Both the Revd E Maule Cole, at Wetwang from 1865 till 1911, and the Revd W H Fox at Thixendale from 1870 till 1911, had spent almost their whole ministerial life in one parish and 'died in harness'. Thereafter it became rare for any incumbent to stay in one

parish for longer than ten years. Shortish incumbencies and long interregna is the story of the High Wolds parishes in the 20th century.

The vicar of Fridaythorpe from 1906 to 1917 was Rev Walter Turner who was married with two daughters and lived in the vicarage. He was better known for writing humorous Yorkshire Dialect; one of his better known books was titled "Goodies". He died in his forties and is buried in Fridaythorpe churchyard. With the death of Sir Tatton Sykes II in 1913, the power of Sledmere was eclipsed. His heir, Sir Mark Sykes, arranged that a bust of his father should be placed in each of the churches he had built or restored. They can still be seen, powerful reminders of a time that was past. For since 1913 not only have much of the more outlying parts of the Sledmere estate been sold but the fact that the new baronet was, like his mother, a fervent Roman Catholic brought to an abrupt end the practical concern of the Sykes family for the well-being of the local churches and the building of the beautiful Roman Catholic chapel in the restored Sledmere House. Architecturally this has possibly had a beneficent effect: the clock stopped for our five 'Sykes' churches in 1913 and since then almost nothing has changed. The three great chandeliers now hang in Sledmere church, but they were part of the original plan, and the high altar edged forward at Wetwang, but visually this can hardly be noticed; otherwise Rip van Winkle reigns. If you want to know what a typical Anglican Parish Church looked like a hundred years ago come to the High Wolds! Though visually this is very soothing it may not be the best witness to a vibrant church life.

And we need only to step downhill to Acklam and Leavening to find a contrasting way forward. For here we will find the two most user-friendly churches in the High Wolds. At Acklam, after the demolition of their huge and remote parish church in 1972, the congregation were able to take over the former Wesleyan Chapel at the heart of the village. This simple building of 1794 now makes the perfect church for a small village.

Things get even better when we come to Leavening. There the school of 1850 is now the parish church of the Venerable Bede and is shared with the Methodists with comfortable chairs, good heating, a kitchen and toilets. Despite the splendours of Sledmere and the long histories of our ancient parish churches, Leavening  must get the accolade for 'The Best Church in the High Wolds'.

Huggate

Aerial view of Wold House Farm in the 1960s which shows the fold yard and stable block. A block of wagon sheds with grainary (granary) above is off the photograph to the left. This was a typical layout of a Wolds farm. The outside privy is the small building to the right of the house.

Huggate Dikes – a good example of Bronze Age earthworks which form part of a more extensive system. There are many theories regarding the reason for their construction – perhaps a land boundary or drovers' route connecting to Millington. Originally the troughs would have been much deeper and therefore the banks much higher. This really shows what 'manpower' can achieve; the digging would probably have been done with deer shoulder blades!

Looking north down the main street towards the church with the school behind the tree and the joiner's shop next to Blyth's pond, which was used for watering animals.

St Mary's church dates from the 13th century. The tower and spire were built a century later. The east window was installed in 1884 as a memorial to James Christie. It was paid for by tenants of his Huggate estate. The Rectory on the left, now Kirkdale House, was built in 1863.

Huggate school – 1955.

Back row: Geoffrey Bailey, ?, Susan Hara, Michael Preston, George Snowden, Ian Stocks, Mary Roe, Diane Stocks, Jeanette Witty, Mrs Cass
Front row: ?, May Nelson, Susan Stocks, Margaret Bailey, Susan Hollingsworth, Stephen Peck.

Reverend Jones with James Watts, his groom/handyman, in front of the vicarage.

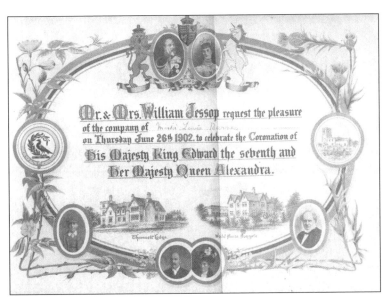

Invitation from Mr & Mrs Jessop, owners of the Huggate Estate, to Master Lewis Barnes to attend the celebrations to mark the coronation of Edward VII. It shows Huggate Wold house at the bottom right, and their home, Thornsett Lodge, near Sheffield, where they owned steelworks.

Ladies cricket team 1950s.

Elsie Sissons, Mollie Line, Hazel Kirby, Win Keeling, Rose Goodwin
Front: Agnes Dawson, Ivy Cooper, Mable Jones, Lorna Tindale, Odette Lister.

Water carriers collecting water from the Mar pond. Mere Farm is the house behind the Mar pond. Harold and Lillian Noble lived there. Harold was a carrier and brought things from Middleton station including fish and coal. He also had a threshing set. They ran a fish and chip shop from the house.

The two semi-detached houses, now Walnut Cottage, and Island House at the west end of the village.

Looking north down the main street. Church Farm and Hemsworth Farm are on the left, the school wall is on the right.

Looking down the main street towards the village green and Manor Farm beyond. The small building attached to the whitewashed house on the left became the tailor's shop. The building to the right of it was the original Wesleyan chapel, you can see the bricked up windows. Joseph Smith, a Methodist minister deemed it not big enough. He embarked on a preaching tour to raise funds to build a larger one. (see 'Chapels')

A later photograph of Tailor's House and Mr Barnes' tailor's shop, which closed in the 1960s. The apprentices lived above the shop. One of those apprentices was Amos Hoggard, father of Leslie and John. He married the tailor, William Barnes' daughter. The business was carried on by his son, 'Bunny' Barnes until it closed in the 1960s.

Hemsworth Cottages and the village shop and post office. The shop, run by John and Audrey Hoggard for many years, sold virtually everything; if they didn't have it, they could get it!

The Wolds Inn. The garage on the right is now part of the dining room; the stables on the left have been converted to accommodation. The chapel on the left of the photograph was converted to a house by Harry and May Elvidge when they retired from running the inn.

Sissons' House, Silver Street. The two houses where the Sissons and Pennock families lived on Silver Street are now one house, Badger Cottage. The Post van stands outside.

Huggate School and adjoining schoolmaster's house. The school closed in 1960 and both buildings have now been converted into one house. Church Farm is the white building in the background and the corner of Church Row can be seen on the left.

Looking towards Eastland Farm with Manor Farm on the left. The site of Huggate well can be seen fenced off on the village green. The well is the second deepest well in England at 339ft.

'Eastlands' was built by the Jessop family and was used as a shooting lodge. A former chalk house on this site was lived in by a well-known local Methodist preacher, Joseph Smith, who referred to it as 'The Huggate Farm' in his book 'Memoir of Joseph Smith of South Holme'. He lived in Huggate from 1873-1883.

Harry Elvidge, postman, delivers the mail despite the snow in February 1940. He was also the publican of the Wolds Inn, driver of the school bus, drove the darts teams to matches in other local pubs and he ran a small-holding and a taxi service.

Chapels

By Chris Whitfield

John Wesley had been an ordained minister in the Church of England when in 1738 he had a conversion experience in Aldergate Street in London, when to use his own words, "I felt my heart strangely warmed". From then on, he began his preaching ministry, much of it outdoors and riding on horseback throughout the country. Sometimes he was barred from preaching in churches although he remained in the Church of England to his dying day. He died in 1791 and his brother Charles who wrote so many of the hymns, pre-deceased him and died in 1788.

John Wesley first visited Driffield in 1772; his journal records that on "Thursday 23rd June, about 11, I preached at Driffield. The sun was extremely hot but I was tolerably screened by a shady tree". Tradition says that the "shady tree" was an elm tree that stood in the Market Place.

It is possible that there may have been followers of John Wesley in Driffield before this visit of 1772, as he had preached at Bridlington on 20th June 1770, but we do know that after his visit a small society was formed. The early Wesleyan Methodists would meet in houses or outbuildings until they were able to build a church. Their first Chapel in Driffield was built in Westgate in 1795 which was 23 years after the visit of Mr Wesley.

The Primitive Methodists or "Ranters" as they were often called were a breakaway from the Wesleyan Methodists. Hugh Bourne and William Clowes were converted to the Christian Faith in the early 1800s and on the 31st May 1807 the first Camp Meeting was held at Mow Cop in Staffordshire. Camp Meetings were an idea from the USA and introduced a man named Lorenzo Dow. The meeting lasted for most of the day and many speakers took part and many Prayer Meetings were an important feature of the proceedings. Another Camp Meeting was held at Mow Camp in 1810 and after this William Clowes began his missionary work. In 1819, the Nottingham Circuit sent him to Hull and on 24th May he also preached in York and many societies were formed in the area. As with the early Wesleyans, homes and outbuildings were used for worship. And also, again like the Wesleyans, many ladies were found amongst the early preachers. It is remarkable that 150 years later their Mother Church (the Church of England) was still arguing about the suitability of women to be vicars!

In 1821 William Clowes was appointed to open a Mission in Scarborough and the first primitive Methodist Chapel was opened at St Sepulchre Street on November 25th 1821. The first preaching plan for Scarborough contained 12 names of which 3 were women. On his way to Scarborough in January 1821, Mr Clowes had preached at various places en route, of which Driffield was one.

To quote from Henry Woodcock's book of 1889 " Primitive Methodism on the Yorkshire Wolds" (PMOTYW); the early Primitive Methodists "were men and women of consecrated lives, and by their plodding industry and untiring energy, they kept the neighbourhood alive with religious excitement, walking ability, strength of lungs, strong faith, warm hearts, plain language and impassioned ardour".

Such a one was John Oxtoby who was born at Little Givendale in 1762. At the age of 37 he was converted and joined the Wesleyans. In 1818 he met William Clowes in Hull and joined the Primitives and became one of their greatest preachers having a great influence on the Yorkshire Wolds. Renowned for the great emphasis he placed on prayer he was known as Praying Johnny. He is buried in Warter Churchyard and his grave stone was refurbished in recent years.

Due to the enclosure of the early 1800s the population of the Wolds' villages sometimes more than doubled in the early years from 1800 onwards, with many reaching their peak about the 1870s. Men were needed to do the manual work on the farms and maids to help with the work in the farm houses. Also many tradesmen were required in the villages to supply the needs of the rising population.

It was often said that the Church of England attracted the Squire and the wealthy farmers, and the Primitive Methodists attracted the farm workers and maids. Although this may have been a generalisation there was also a lot of truth in it.

Reverend Henry Woodcock records that on the Driffield Primitive Methodist Plan in the 1800s there were 75 local preachers which comprised:

3 Blacksmiths
2 Carriers
1 Dressmaker
5 Farmers
24 Farm Workers
1 Gentleman
8 Grocers
3 Pig-jobbers
1 Rag Merchant
3 Railway Employees
1 Wool Merchant
6 Shoemakers
6 Tea Dealers
2 Tailors
3 Wheelwrights
6 Woodmen

Pig-jobbers were dealers in pigs, and I find the title very appealing.

The way in which the preachers travelled to conduct their services changed over the years. John Wesley obviously travelled on horseback because his was a nationwide ministry covering many miles.

In the early years of the 19th Century most ministers and local preachers would walk, and sometimes the journeys were long due to the fact that Circuits were larger in the early days. Towards the end of the 19th Century most Circuits obtained a horse and trap. From Driffield, the centre of the Circuit, 4 or 5 preachers would be set out and a preacher would be dropped off in each village on the way with the driver going to the furthermost Chapel and collecting his fellow local preachers on his return. The horses had a reputation for being very old, very thin and very slow. Two local preachers were talking about them one day and the conversation went thus – "Ah see we've getten some acetylene lamps fer t'circuit trap" – to which the other local preacher replied – "we've had a set o lean hosses a lang wahle".

The story is also told of the horse and trap on its way back to Driffield. The old horse was going slowly from one side of the road to the other as it climbed the hill out of Sledmere, not fast enough for Brother Scott who said "Gee Up", upon which the horse stopped stone dead. His fellow preacher said, "Noo Thou's blown leet out".

The Circuit moved on to cars in the early to mid 1900s with the drivers dropping off preachers at each village and collecting them on their way back from their preaching appointments.

Things changed little in the years to the war which began in 1914. Agriculture suffered years of depression from time to time and after the First World War things were never to be the same again. Some men were conscripted, many others volunteered, but as can be seen on our War Memorials many never returned.

In 1932 the three Methodist Churches in the country united. Although in the High Wold villages we only had the Wesleyan Methodists and the Primitive Methodists, there was also a smaller group called the United Methodists or Free Methodists who had a lovely Chapel in Bridge Street in Driffield. A few Chapels in Hull, Holderness and one in Westgate, Driffield did not join the Union and remained as Primitive Methodists. In the Union of 1932 most villages kept their Wesleyan and Primitive Chapels, some sharing alternative Sundays for worship and others closing as time went by.

By the start of the Second World War in 1939, mechanisation was making its presence felt. During the 1940s the Shire horse was quickly phased out and the tractor and other machinery took over. In the next 60 years or so the need for men to work on the farms and maids in the farmhouse, and the small traders, quickly diminished. As these were the people who had formed the Methodist congregations – so it was that many of the Chapels closed for the lack of members; as did many other organisations, due to social change.

Many of these Chapels had no great beauty in an architectural sense and had cost little to build, although they were greatly loved by the worshippers at the time. Many, especially, the Primitive Methodist Chapels, had been opened bearing a debt because few of their members were wealthy. Many of the buildings could best be described as "barn like" and although the Wesleyan Chapels were generally finer buildings, they too could be easily converted into village halls or houses, as in these examples at Huggate, Sledmere and Thixendale.

So we come to the individual villages of the High Wolds. Wetwang, Sledmere, Fridaythorpe and Fimber belong to the Driffield Circuit, whilst Huggate and Thixendale belonged to Pocklington Circuit, and Acklam belonged to Malton Circuit. It is reasonable to assume that those Chapels in the Driffield Circuit would be influenced by the happenings in Hull, Bridlington and Scarborough, whilst those in the Pocklington Circuit by happenings in York.

Now for the individual villages:

Acklam – Although a meeting house was established in Acklam in 1790, the first chapel, a Wesleyan, was built in 1794 which is much earlier than any other village in the High Wolds.

Interestingly this early chapel still survives and although it closed as a Methodist Church in 1966, it now continues as an Anglican Church. This must be one of the few places in the country where this has happened. A Primitive Methodist Chapel was built here in 1821, which was again very early, but this closed and became a stable. Apparently this Chapel cost £105.00 to build and opened with a debt of £60.00. The population of the village in the 1880s was 207 and the membership was 25 but surprisingly no Sunday School for the children (most probably the Wesleyans had one).

Leavening – The first Primitive Chapel was built in 1821 and re-built in 1849 at a cost of £100 with a debt of £65. In the 1880s the population is recorded at 391, of which 48 were members of the Primitive Methodist Chapel and 28 children attended the Sunday School. The Wesleyan Chapel here was built in 1824 and is still in use as a church shared by the Methodists and Church of England.

Wetwang's first Chapel was built in 1812 and was a Wesleyan Chapel which in 1886 became a Sunday School until 1964. It was then a store for a few years and was then converted into a flat and village shop.

Another Wesleyan Chapel was built in 1886, closed in 1964 and demolished in 1978.

A Primitive Methodist Chapel was built in 1824, rebuilt in 1870 (whether on the same piece of ground we know not), closed in 1959 and demolished in 1961.

The present St Paul's Methodist Chapel was built in 1964 on land bought from Mr George Paul (at a kindly reduced price). The architect was Mr Bernard Blanchard who later became a Methodist Minister.

We sometimes think all was sweetness and light in the "Good Old Days" but I remember when Mrs Leppington was the organist and two sisters in law, Mrs Prince and Mrs Priest sat to her right. They had a big fall out, so the organ had to be moved so one could sit at one side of Mrs Leppington and one at the other. Also the prayer meetings were well renowned, but they did say that Jess (Jessyman) Wiles always had the same prayer, "Plunged in a Gulf of Deep Despair, Plunge us Agean Lord". Hardly something to look forward to!

Fimber – The Wesleyan Chapel was rebuilt in 1863 at a cost of £200 and demolished in 1948. During the Second World War a German bomber jettisoned its bombs in and around Fimber and one of these bombs caused damage to this Chapel. The Primitive Chapel was built in 1839 and rebuilt in 1863 at a cost of £198 before being closed in 1967 and demolished in 1975.

It was said that around 1820 Fimber was notorious for dog fighting, badger baiting and cricket, and if during the working day a badger could be found or a cricket match arranged the ploughs were left in the furrow or the flails on the barn floor. Rev Henry Woodcock records in "Primitive Methodism on the Yorkshire Wolds" that after the preaching of John Oxtoby (Praying Johnny), many of the ringleaders were converted and their sports abolished – but obviously not cricket!

Fridaythorpe – A Wesleyan Chapel was built in 1840, closed in the 1970s and soon after demolished. Parts of the walls still remain.

The Primitive Methodist Chapel was built in 1857 at a cost of £128 with £28 of debt outstanding. In the late 1800s it had 22 members with a similar sized Sunday School. This Chapel was in Pocklington Circuit whilst the Wesleyan Chapel was in Driffield Circuit.

The Rev S Loxton tells that once, when walking to Fridaythorpe the weather was remarkably fine, when suddenly he saw wild geese flying overhead, a sure sign to Woldsmen of approaching storm. The geese were true guides; on his return the snow was so deep that the roads were not discoverable and the storm so violent that he had to grope his way under the hedges and arrived at Huggate exhausted. Here a doctor invited him to take a seat in a carriage and so he arrived safely at Pocklington. Many a Wolds preacher has passed through similar scenes and cherished recollections of the kindness of friends in giving them a ride when walking was almost impossible.

Huggate's first Wesleyan Chapel was built in 1837 and closed in 1885 and is now a house. A new Wesleyan Chapel was built in 1885 to accommodate 300 people at a cost of £480. It closed in 1974 and is now also a house.

The Primitive Chapel was built in 1849 and demolished in the 1980s. The cost of this Chapel was £180 and the debt was £100 on opening which seems a large percentage. Surprisingly the population for Huggate in the 1880s is recorded as 550. The membership of the Chapel was 33 with a similar number of Sunday School children.

Sledmere has one of the most interesting stories to tell. As an estate village there was always a clash between the Squire, the Vicar and the local Methodists. Although no Chapel was built until 1889 the Wesleyans met in a laundry on a farm occupied by Mr Hicks. The first class meeting was formed by Mr Sellars, a local Primitive Methodist preacher from Pocklington. In the 1820s the first Sir Tatton Sykes threatened tenants with dismissal from their holdings if they entertained the Methodist preachers; some gave in but others stuck to their convictions. Tom Hope, in whose house, preaching services were held stood firm. One day Sir Tatton said "If you don't turn out those Methodist preachers you'll have to give up your holding". Tom, who had the courage of his convictions said, "You have been a good landlord to me Sir Tatton, and I should not like to lose my holding. I will do almost anything to please you but God has blessed me under the Primitive Methodists and I'll never leave them or turn them out". Sir Tatton replied "well you're a good sort of fellow, Tom, and you shall have a bit more land". Others also resisted the threats of their employers; many of them clung to Methodism at the risk of their jobs, which meant losing their bread and butter.

Before the Chapels were built both the Wesleyans and the Primitives met in houses and outbuildings. The Primitives had three preaching places, one in the village, one at Pry Cottages and one at Mill Cottages. Quoting from PMOTYW (page 135), "the second Sir Tatton Sykes has always treated our people with more than kindly toleration. He has never debarred them from any rights and privileges because they were Methodists".

Reverend C Leafe in 1889 asked Sir Tatton for land on which to build a Chapel. He kindly offered to give a good site but the Methodists could only proceed if the Vicar was willing. When asked, the Vicar said "I am surprised you ask such a favour. Before we left College, we were made to swear we would never allow a Methodist Chapel to be erected in a Parish of which we had charge". Rev Leafe then told the Vicar "There are about 50 men and women praying about it and it has been revealed to me in prayer that if you stand in the way of us getting land to build a Chapel the Lord will take you out of the world". What a threat! In a couple of days the Vicar came back with his answer "That he would not stand in the way".

The Primitive Methodist Chapel, built by W Petch of Middleton, opened in 1889 and is still in use.

The Wesleyan Chapel built also in 1889 closed and is now a private dwelling.

Thixendale – Of all the seven villages, it is the only one which didn't contain both Primitive and Wesleyan Chapels. It belonged to the Pocklington Circuit and although in the 1890s Driffield Circuit had 26 villages with Primitive Methodist Chapels, Pocklington and Malton Circuits only had three each in the Wolds villages.

The only Chapel at Thixendale was the Wesleyan Chapel, built in 1837 and which was restored in 1906 and closed in 1974. This has been restored and is now a house after being used as a stable. I remember taking a service there in the 1960s (most probably a Harvest Festival) and the faithfulness of people like Mrs Welburn and Tom Hudson who later became a local preacher.

Reviewing the history of the Wolds Chapels has brought back many memories. After John Wesley's great journeys on horseback preaching the good news about Jesus there were many preachers who followed; many walking many miles to take services. I suppose you could say they knew of no other way so readily accepted it. I remember George Ford from Tibthorpe, preaching at Wetwang in the 1940s telling us that one night when it was blowing a gale and very wet, he said to his wife "Ah deeant think ah's gaain to go ti preach ti nite so shah sez ti me, "come here an get thi coat on an gan. Tho isn't gaain ti be a butterfly preacher". Even in the 1940s and 1950s some of our local preachers were using broad Yorkshire in the pulpit and of course everyone could understand them. I also remember George Ford telling us of a man called Colley at Langtoft who was a regular at services. George Ford said that if he was asked for his opinion of the service he would say "Oh it was alright, but ah cud ov deean better missen". George said one stormy night the preacher didn't turn up so I said to him, "Now's yer chance Colley, up in ti pulpit". So we had a hymn, a prayer, a hymn, two lessons, another hymn and the notices, another hymn and then he came to the sermon "I am the Good Shepherd" he says and then silence. "I am the Good Shepherd", then silence, so he says again "I am the Good Shepherd" but he couldn't go on so I said to him "Cum down out o' there Colley, thou'll do better amang thi flock".

When George told his stories he always made them fit into what he was saying. I am sure the congregations didn't mind as long as what they preached on Sundays they did in the week and the message came from the heart, and their Christian experience.

How we can look back with fond memories to the Methodist year. Wonderful services on Good Friday and Easter Day, Sunday School Anniversaries so brilliantly remembered by Arthur Jarrett in his dialect poem "Sundah Skeeal Anniverssory". Chapel Anniversaries, service 2.15pm followed by ham salad (real Yorkshire ham) teas. Evening service followed by supper. Then Harvest

Festival with the sale on Monday after the service and later still, Christmas singing round the village and farms.

FOND MEMORIES INDEED!

Leavening

c mid 1930s – Looking west up Main Street from Beck Lane. The two cottages on the left hand side have since been converted into one, now called Gannow. Ice cream and sweets were sold from the cottage on the right hand side.

1930s – View looking west across Leavening. In the 1930s, Wold Terrace was built on the site of Woodland House (bottom left). Later the row of cottages in the foreground was demolished to make way for more modern housing.

Date unknown – East end of Main Street. Third door on the left was the entrance of Mrs Maud Turpie's post office and shop in the late 1920s to 1930s. Later she took over the shop premises further up Main Street (now a private house called The Old Post Office). The gable end wall of Woodland House can be seen at the junction of Beck Lane. On the right is the Wesleyan Methodist Chapel built in 1824. It was sold and became a private house in 2007.

Early 1900s – View of the junction of Beck Lane with Main Street and Dam Lane. The house in the foreground is Woodland House. The road to Leavening Brow went directly behind Woodland House.

Early 1900s – Cottages, The Brow. At the time of the photo Samuel & Hannah Binge lived in one cottage and Thomas & Elizabeth Binge lived in the other. Samuel was a threshing machine proprietor born in Kirkham. Thomas was a traction engine driver born in Brawby. Their wives were from Leavening. Samuel was the father of Tom and Motty Binge who are still remembered travelling around the local farms with their threshing sets. It is now a single dwelling. Most recently Johnny Corner lived in the house until he died in 2011.

1908 – The Board Inn, now called the Jolly Farmer. In the Census records, John Harrison was the beer house keeper and grocer from 1871 to 1911. He was from Acklam. The appearance of Manor Farm on the left has changed little to the present day.

1908 – View of The Board Inn from Sunnybank. Note there were dwellings to the right of the beer house. On the far right is Hallgarth Farm which was farmed by Mrs Elizabeth Walker and her family. The Walker family had lived there from about 1860. One of her sons, Mark Walker, later farmed at Brook Cottage on Beck Lane with his wife Maud.

1900–1910 – Peterkin's shop on Main Street. This was to the right of Manor Farm on the north side of the street. The building is no longer standing. Mr John Peterkin is the elderly man behind the wooden railings; in Kelly's Directory 1879, he was recorded as a grocer in the village. Later he was also a draper. His son, Eli Peterkin, took over the business in the late 1890s/1900, and was still running the shop in 1937.

1930s – The crossroads at Golden Well, looking along Dam Lane. The house was also called Golden Well and it was said to have been the police house. In 1901 Mr John Peterkin, retired grocer, was living there with his wife, Mary. Mr Wilson Lamb lived in Golden Well from 1939 until his death in 2004; his wife, Annie, died in 1988. He was a well known character who kept Jersey cows, and sold butter and eggs from the house. The pinfold was on the corner of Dam Lane and the road to Acklam.

1951 – Harvest at Southfield Farm.

Left to right: Harold Varey, Mr Adams, Brian Paul, Billy Paul.

1930s/1940s – The Primitive Methodist Chapel, Main Street. The chapel was officially opened on 8th October 1820 by Mr John Verity, a noted preacher from the Pocklington Circuit. It used to be well attended with around 100 worshippers at the afternoon service and 35 in Sunday school. However by the early 1950s it had become a joiner's shop run by Mr Grimshaw Fowler. Later it was used as a barn. Now a bungalow, Bryn Cottage, stands on the site. The railings can still be seen.

Early 1950s – Crossroads. Southfields Farm is in the centre of the picture with its barns and orchard behind.

c1900 – Sunnybank Farm. In 1920s and 1930s Mr Christopher Bogg, and later his widow Mrs Mary Bogg, ran a shop from the right hand side cottage. Mr Bogg's elderly mother lived in the left hand side cottage. It is now a farm run by Robert Holtby and his family; he is one of Harold Varey's grandsons.

c1907 – The old school built in 1850 for 76 children. It was also used as a chapel of ease for Acklam Church. After 1907, the building was used as a village institute. On 31st October 1965 it was rededicated as a church to The Venerable Bede. In 2009 it became the joint place of worship for both the Anglicans and the Methodists following extensive renovation work.

c1907 – The public elementary school shortly after opening. It was erected in 1907 for 100 children. The average attendance in 1913 was 75. The girls' hats alone are worth a closer look; the Tam o'Shanters could be made by following a simple knitting pattern.

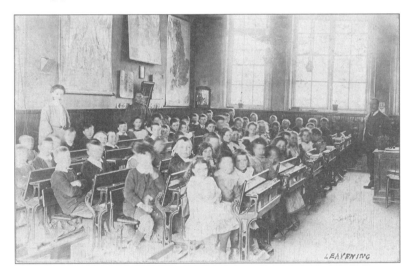

c1907 – Inside the new school. The man on the right is William Grassby who was the school master. He was originally from Leeds and the son of a joiner. Records show that he was the school master from 1888 until 1922. Previously he had taught in Staffordshire.

1935 – In the school yard. Rehearsals for the Silver Jubilee Display to celebrate 25 years of King George V's reign. The building behind the maypole is the school house.

Left to Right: Joyce Trousdale, Ruth Paul, Myra Midgley, Rosie Varey, Flora Peterkin, Jean Stevens, Dorothy Midgley (behind), Margaret Peterkin, Kathleen Stevens, Gladys Peterkin, Alice Milburn, Pamela Walsh

c1910 – George Varey of Southfield Farm with his son, Harold, on Leppington Lane. The water mill is on the left and the mill dam is on the right behind the cart. The mill was run by John Milburn who was also the carrier to York. His descendant Peter Milburn now lives in the house. Although it is no longer a working mill, the pipe that fed the mill can still be seen in the garden.

c1907 – The Hare And Hounds, York Road. Mrs Hannah King was the licencee between 1892 and 1913. Mrs King used to hold The Hare Supper on Guy Fawkes Night; it was a tradition dating back to at least the early 19th century. The hares were provided by Lord Middleton. The Oddfellows Club Feast was held in a marquee in a field belonging to Mr King.

Left to right: James King, son, Thomas, Maud, Alice, Mrs Annie King, daughter in law, Mary, Mrs Hannah King.

c1908 – York Road looking east. Building in foreground is the mill. The sign for the Hare Hounds can be seen further up the road. The forge is next to the Hare and Hounds; the blacksmith was Samuel Stevens and his son George was later to take over the business. The house at the top is the farmhouse which originally belonged to Boundales Farm and was owned by Mr Preston of Burythorpe House.

Acknowledgments:

Don Howarth, for all the hard work collecting the photographs and research that resulted in 'Leavening through the ages'.

And many thanks to all the residents of Leavening who have been so helpful, in particular Mrs Mary Lee.

References:

'Leavening through the ages' – Don Howarth

'The changing years' – Tom Midgley. Written by Ruth Beckett 1993

'Reflections on the changing years' – Tom Midgley. Written by Ruth Beckett 2000

High Wolds Village Schooling

By Trevor Smith

Early Days

In the village of Fimber, around 1830, in a small candlelit room half a dozen very small children were learning their alphabet and numbers, using a few slates and chalk. The teacher was a labouring man's daughter known as 'Aunty Jane', probably Jane Medd who taught in her father's cottage. To further their education some of these children may then have attended a school in Fridaythorpe run by a woman named Mrs Barker – again, a labourer's wife who taught from the front room of her cottage. Teaching such as this was common in the early 19th century and before, carried out by a villager, the local vicar, curate, or on occasions, by peripatetic schoolmasters hired by the squire or parson to teach for a short while and then move on. The quality of this teaching is unknown but the Reverend Curtis of Huggate, in a school building grant application, was very clear in his views when he described existing educational provision in the village as 'very inadequate' and kept by a 'very incompetent master in a private room'[1]. The moral standing of these early teachers could also be in doubt as with one 19th century Huggate teacher, Thomas White, convicted for poaching and sentenced to prison unless he paid a substantial fine – not the best example to local children.

We only get glimpses of pre 19th century education in our villages from sources such as Archbishops' Visitation Reports, which identified the level of Dissenter worship and how Church of England's status was being affected. One of the questions asked was on village education and replies show there was a school in Acklam in 1600 and Sledmere in 1596, the latter being run by Schoolmaster Thomas Ogle. At a later date in Sledmere 'Richard Sykes built a Schoolhouse at one end of the ha-ha to the south of the Hall in 1750' but this was demolished in 1778 and 'evidently replaced in the 1780s by a building combining a schoolroom

---

1   Huggate School Records, NS/7/1/5590, Church of England Record Centre

and Master's house' south west of Sledmere House.[2] For Fridaythorpe there is a school recorded in 1744 and in Wetwang Thomas Waite, the ejected vicar and his wife were said to have kept a school from the early 1660s and the Sykes family contributed to the salary of a schoolmaster from 1790. One record in Archbishop Drummond's Visitation of 1764 identifies the following in Acklam;

> *There is a school built at the expense of the inhabitants endowed with an acre of land...The vicar and Overseers of the Poor are for the time being trustees. Two poor children are taught English ....The Master's name is George Jennings, Parish Clerk and as such licensed'*[3]

Funding for these early schools came from local squires, such as the Sykes', contributing to buildings or from charitable donations. One example of the latter was Mrs Francis Barker who left £30 in her will in 1729 for a school in Acklam and three years earlier £50 for poor relief and education in Huggate, the village in which her father had been Rector. However leaving this money did not always guarantee a school be set up as the Charity accounts show there was no teacher in Huggate between 1730 –64.[4] Sometimes it was parents who paid for schooling such as in Fridaythorpe in 1818 where 30 pupils were supported in this way. Occasionally, such as with Charles Sellars in Fridaythorpe, money was left in a will to be given to the children, in this case for good attendance ranging from 1s to 10s.

Nineteenth Century Progress

It was during the 19th century that public interest in education increased due in part to a growing population and the increase in religious evangelism. The result was a number of Educational Acts being put on the statute book, culminating

---

2   D&S Neave, *Victoria History of the Counties of England, Yorkshire East Riding, vol.VIII: Sledmere and the Northern Wolds,* Boydelle & Brewer, 2008, p.196.

3   C Annesley & P Hoskin, *Archbishop Drummond's Visitation Return 1764,* Borthwick Calendars 21, 2001, p.5.

4   J. Lawson, *Primary Education in East Yorkshire, 1560 – 1902,* East Yorkshire History Society, Series 10, p.10.

in the 1870 Elementary Education Act (the Forster Act), which set a framework for the teaching of children from the age of 5 to 13. Later Acts extended the age range and introduced free education, as a result of these, and the interest in education from bodies such as the National Society for Promoting the Education of the Poor in the Principles of the Established Church, there was considerable increase in building schools, including the High Wolds villages.

School Building

Many of the buildings built in the 19th century were architecturally very simple being made up of one or two rooms built of brick with slate roofs, basic toilet facilities and sometimes Master's accommodation attached.

The photograph shows Thixendale school and schoolhouse which were completed in 1876.

In Huggate the dimensions of the schoolroom were 36 feet long, 18 feet wide and 12 feet high – not much space to accommodate and teach 80 – 90 children of all different ages. Built in 1872 with six rooms for the Master and his family, the total cost is shown in the following balance sheet.

As can be seen £375 was raised locally – something of a battle for Reverend Curtis – £80 coming as a grant from the National Society and £80 from interest on an endowment. Clearly a lot of local money went into the project but in other villages where the Sykes family were landowners it would appear they were prepared to provide the necessary funds for schools in Fimber, Wetwang and Sledmere.

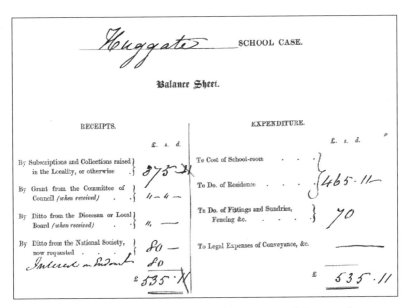

1871 Statement of Costs for National Society[5]

Unfortunately many of these schools closed during the 20th century due mainly to falling class sizes, including Fimber in 1948, Fridaythorpe 1984 and Huggate 1960. Acklam closed in 1947 due to it being structurally unsound and sold to the village for £250 in 1960 for use as a Church Hall. The photograph below was taken in 1963/64 after Thixendale School closed and merged with Fridaythorpe School.

Teachers

'Wackford Squeers' perhaps, influences our view of the quality of Victorian teachers with his 'practical mode of teaching' an example of which was 'bottiney, noun substantive, a knowledge of plants.'[6] Perhaps a parody but we do know

---

5   Huggate School Records, SL59/1, Treasure House, Beverley

6   Charles Dickens, *Nicholas Nickleby,* Wordsworth Classics, 1995, p.86.

Back row: Gillian Stark, Susan Midgley, Kevin Stainforth, George Patrick, Chris Wilmot, Andrew Stark, David Hewitt, Clifford West, Deborah Longstaff, Heather MacDonald.

Second row: Linda MacDonald, David Lawson, Adrian Brader, John Davis, Alec Moore, Stephen Lyus, Graham Owston, Charles Brader, John West, Kathryn Pexton.

Third row: Richard Megginson, Christine Smith, Catherine Longstaff, ? Megginson, Mark Jagger, Deborah Megginson, Colin Stainforth.

Front row: Jane Ackroyd, Raymond Welburn, Eunice Metcalfe, Angela Patrick, Janet Stavley, Sandra Hewitt, Nigel Wilmot.

that teachers in the latter part of the 19th century were subject to regular Government and Diocesan Inspection and overseen by a local Management Board, often made up of the wealthier villagers and the local Rector. The Master's wife often looked after the girls' education, and in some cases their children were employed as Pupil Teachers, as were Alfred Skelton's three children in Huggate. We have other information on the teachers such as in Thixendale;

March 29th 1888 – Mr Williamson resigned the mastership of the school this day, after nearly 40 years charge of it. He receives a Government pension of £20 per annum on retiring.

April 9th 1888. Monday – Mr Benjamin Schofield commenced his duties today, as the new School-Master. He is from the York Diocesan Training College. His sister is to take the sewing class for girls.

3rd October 1891- Mr Benjamin Schofield having resigned the Mastership of the School, left the village, together with his mother and sister, who had instructed the girls in sewing.

This quick turnover was not uncommon with Huggate having seven different teacher between 1872 and 1888. In Fimber we have the following on teachers;

By 1861, Mary Sawdon, aged 46 at that time, had become the local schoolmistress and her son, Frank, aged 12, was one of 39 school children in Fimber village. Mary, who was born in Thixendale, would have been the first mistress of the new school, endowed by Sir Tatton Sykes, which opened in 1865. Mary retired in 1873 and Elizabeth Jane Wood was appointed schoolmistress in January 1874.

Many teachers did not have formal training but the growing trend towards the end of the century was for teachers to go through the Diocesan Training Colleges such as St Maurice's on Lord Mayors Walk in York, now St John's University.

Crime and Punishment

'Squeers fell upon the boy and caned him soundly; not leaving indeed, until his arm was tired out'.[7] Perhaps a popular perception of Victorian Schools but how true was it? We know from Huggate that poacher/teacher Mr White's answer to recalcitrant children was to pop them 'into the big green bag which held the fiddle' and hang them up on the wall of the schoolhouse. Apparently the children preferred a 'sound beating to that novel punishment'. Proof of the Squeer's approach to punishment is evidenced by Alfred Skelton in Huggate in the 1890s when he records in the School Log Book;

'Had to cane Simpson Allison for rudeness and inattention after being repeatedly cautioned without effect'[8]

---

7   *Nicholas Nickleby*, p. 89 – 90.

8   Huggate School Records, SL59/1

Another problem faced by village schools in the high Wolds was that the children regularly worked on local farms, but this was perhaps understandable 'When the majority of people lived near the subsistence level, every child in the family had to earn his bread as soon as he was capable of doing so'.[9] Children helped with weeding, harvesting, gleaning, flinting or, if not on the land, staying at home to look after the younger children whilst the parents were working. Clearly every penny counted in what was poorly paid, and often short termed, agricultural employment.

What was taught

Thixendale School timetable for 1900 shows subjects divided into Standards set by Government and used as the basis for measuring performance during their Inspections.

One can imagine the difficulty in teaching all the subjects with up to 80 children of different ages and ability in one or two small rooms. The writing was usually done on slates and if broken would often have to be paid for by the child or his family. Geography was simple, relying on a few maps or reading reports of expeditions to far flung places from newspapers, such as Arthur Skelton in Huggate who read to the older boys an article giving 'an account of Lord Lonsdale's expedition to North America'.

---

9   *Primary Education in East Yorkshire, 1560 – 190,* p. 8.

All children participated in learning and singing songs such as "God Bless the Prince of Wales", "The Snail" or "The Swiss Toy", with the infants focussing on animal songs including Mr Spider.

There were sewing classes for the girls who were often divided into two sets with the older children acting as monitors for the juniors, thus providing the Master's wife with much needed support. In the timetable there is reference to Object Lessons which covered writing and speaking on a wide range of topics. In 1875 the agreed subjects included salt, wheels, lock and key, railway station, the sea, and currants and gooseberries.

A later timetable for Thixendale School.

Evacuees

During the Second World War High Wolds village schools opened their doors to children from Hull and Sunderland, who had been moved to avoid German bombing of those cities. Numbers varied with Wetwang taking in 61 evacuees from Sunderland and 54 from Hull and while Fridaythorpe took in 32 evacuees, just two less than the number of local children at the school and Sledmere 40 from Hull and 39 from Sunderland. In Thixendale, the chapel was used as an additional classroom to accommodate the evacuees and their teacher. Part of the school register shows the admission of evacuees from Hull.

Name.	Date of Birth	Hull Sch.	Hull address	Evac. address.	(23)
Perry Kenneth	D 4 : 10 : 34	Hull Rd Sn.	9 Rowley Gr. Ing.L	c/o. Mrs. Wellburn	Thixendale
Harpham Walt.	o 9 : 11 : 27	Hall Rd Sn.	26, 37th Av. N.Hull&d.	c/o. Mrs. Stephen.	"
Lushy. Clifford	o 3 : 6 : 28	" "	2 Weyhlin Gr. "	Raisthorpe Wold.	"
Hardwick Francis	o 27 : 10 : 28	" "	336, Endyke Lane.	c/o Mrs Wellburn	"
Predgeon. John	o 1 : 4 : 28	Courtney St.	2 Victoria I. Beelin St.	Manor Farm .	"
Predgeon. Wm	o 15 : 12 : 29	"	" "	" "	"
Whitfield Brian	o 24 : 7 : 28	Hull Rd Sn.	374 Sylvenie L.	Fotherdale Farm.	"
Moses Alan	o 19 : 4 : 29	" "	123 Deshway as.	Paradise Cottages Fridaythorpe
Sadler John	P 2 : 6 : 35	Fifth Av. Inf.	5, 15th Av. N.Hull &d.	c/o Mrs. Milnes	Burdale
Sadler Sheila	19 : 5 : 33	" " Jun.	" "	"	"
Lundberg Marino	9 : 3 : 31	" " "	32, 32nd Av	Martinholme.	Thixendale
Lundberg Beryl	o 28 : 5 : 35	" " Inf.	" "	"	"
Lyne June.	o 21 : 6 : 31	" " Jun.	81, 21st.	"	c/o. Mrs. Williamson	"
Robinson Audrey	o 4 : 4 : 32	" " Jun.	77, 29th	"	c/o. Mrs. Pudsey.	"
Foston Catherine	o 14 : 9 : 32	" "	22, 26th.	"	c/o. Mrs. Found	"
Tomlinson Mary	o 10 : 10 : 33	" " Jun.	88 21st.	"	c/o. Mr. Williamson	"
Herrison Beryl	o 9 : 6 : 34	" " Inf.	59. 32nd	"	c/o. Mrs. Pudsey.	"
Lushy Dorothy	P 26 : 11 : 30	Hull Rd Jun	2 Weyhlin Gr. N.Hull&d	Raisethorpe Wold	"
Lushy. Beryl	P 6 : 11 : 32	Hull Rd Jun.	" "	"	"
Kettleborough Jean	P. 19 : 11 : 33	Fountain Rd. Inf.	Gton St. St Paul St.	c/o Mrs. Bradley.	"

One can imagine the difference in life styles these evacuees must have experienced but from local recollections it is clear local families in whose houses they stayed made the children very welcome.

The picture below shows evacuees from Pallion School, Sunderland in front of Huggate church.

Of these evacuees all but one left for home after the war. We can only surmise why one girl stayed on in the village – perhaps because her parents died in the bombing. However, some other children who had been evacuated here returned at a later date to live in the area.

It was not only during the war that there was danger from the air. In Huggate the petrol tank of a Mosquito plane, on a training flight in March 1949, crashed into the school porch. Thankfully it was scholarship day and no children were in the school.

Modern Memories

The school memories of villagers in the high Wolds are many and it would be impossible to record them all here by village but the following quotes give a flavour of them;

'Every day we had the milk issue made from powder and water mixed by the older girl, followed by a daily spoon of cod liver oil.'

'The school cleaner did the dinners, which we ate off fold up tables. It cost 2s 6d a week.'

'The Head's dog sat in many of the classes and was often in the school photographs.'

'The Dentist, Mr Jones, called once a year in a caravan and we had free treatment. How we hated him arriving as what he did to our teeth could be called barbaric by today's standards.'

'The school had the Yorkshire Penny Savings Bank and when we had saved a £1 this was entered in the large book.'

'The cloakrooms were separate, desks were of wood which had lift up lids where books pens, rulers etc were kept, with the seat attached for two children.'

'The milk monitors had to go down the village to a local dairy farmer for the milk that each child had a beaker of each morning.'

'Caning was a normal day to day affair if you didn't behave, one teacher would stand at the front of the class flexing a walking stick I think it was to remind us what we'd get if we misbehaved. Another didn't just hit the palms of the hands with a ruler but came down on the palms and up on the knuckles.'

'On average there were over 60 pupils taught by three teachers.'

'One headmaster's wife had some ice skates so when the ice was thick enough on the pond she would take the children who the skates fitted to learn to skate.'

'There were two classes in one room which was divided by a curtain.'

Some children walked nearly two miles to attend school and had to bring their own sandwiches.'

Sledmere

Sledmere Church and Hall

The Church & House

Taken prior to the Great Fire of Sledmere House of May 1911. Sir Tatton's new church stands grandly in the grounds of his country house.

SLEDMERE

Top Row, the School and Methodist Church

Top Row, built in the 1870s, is shown with the brickwork unpainted. The school and schoolhouse were built in 1874/75 and replaced the school on Wetwang road (now Keeper's Cottage). The Primitive Methodist Chapel was built in 1899.

The Estate House and Office

The house, with adjoining Estate Office, was built in 1895. It forms part of a quartet of terracotta brick houses in the centre of the village designed by John Birch.

The Villa. The most grand of the quartet was the Estate Clerk of Works' house completed in 1900.

The Post Office

(Photo courtesy of Bob Beacroft)

The Post Office was built in 1896 on the site of one of the old lodges, which housed the old Post Office. The Wesleyan Chapel to the right was converted into a pair of cottages in 1947.

Sledmere House

(Photo courtesy of Dennis Lazenby)

Note to the left of the picture the servants' wing which was demolished c.1946

The Lodges & Triton Inn. This pair of lodges stood opposite The Triton Inn and were not for the entrance of Sledmere but led to the Croom Estate owned by neighbouring landowners, the Rousby family. Croom was purchased in 1811-12 by Sir Mark Masterman Sykes.

The Blacksmith's Shop   *(Photo courtesy of Edgar Scott)*

The Sledmere Forge stood next to The Triton and was demolished in the early 50's. It was run by the Scotts and was a social meeting place for the old boys of the village and any passing "Wold Rangers".

Bottom Row, Sledmere.

Bottom Row, Bridlington Road. A row of ten cottages built in 1870 replaced those known as Drury's Row.

The Estate Buildings Yard c.1900 *(Photo courtesy of Bob Beacroft)*

At this time there would have been approximately 40 men working in the Buildings Department and as in other departments there was a strict hierarchy.

Queen Eleanor's Monument. Sledmere.

The Eleanor Cross. Designed by Temple Moore and erected in 1896/7 near the village pond. In 1918 Sir Mark Sykes added the engraved brass plaques to the officers and men of the 5th Battalion of the Yorkshire Regiment killed in the First World War. The figure of Sir Mark was added later as a memorial after his death at the Paris Peace Conference in 1919.

THE CASTLE, SLEDMERE.

The Castle. Built in 1778 as an "eye-catcher" to be seen from Sledmere House.

Taking the coffin of Sir Tatton Sykes, 5th Baronet to St Mary's Church. (*Photo courtesy of Dennis Lazenby*). On 5th May 1913 the early morning train from Malton to Sledmere carried Sir Tatton's coffin. It was loaded onto a farm wagon, drawn by a pair of heavy horses, and taken from the station to the church. After a short service the body was to lie in state until the funeral on 9th May.

Buildings Yard Men c1899 (*Photo courtesy of Bob Beacroft*)

Back: Ernest Dobson, Stuart Ellis, Tom Scott, Fred Addison, T Yates

Front: George Train, George Southwick, Harry Train, Robert Beacroft, Harry Brown

Royal Visit   (*Photo courtesy of Edith Harland*)

Dorothy Whitfield and Edith Baker are eagerly awaiting the arrival of King George VI and Queen Elizabeth accompanied by Princess Margaret, at the Lodge gates.

Sledmere Church Choir Members   (*Photo courtesy of Edith Harland*)

Back row: ?, Mrs Sinton, Billy Sygrove, Nellie Bell, ?

Front row: Dorothy Whitfield, Mary Sygrove, Edith Baker, Julia Stubbings, Pauline Sygrove, Michael Sinton, Clive Baker

Village Social

(Photo courtesy of Sheila Robinson)

Back Row: Enid Wilson, Joan Robinson, Joan Robinson

Middle Row: Sheila Robinson, Betty Lazenby, Mrs Cracknel, Mrs Sinton, Mrs Scott, Mrs Southwick, Mrs Heeley, Edith Hague

Front Row: Tom Southwick, Ted Heeley

Sledmere Cricket Club – Winners of the Driffield & District Cup 1920

(Photo courtesy of Clarks of Croome)

Back row: G Dales, W Dales, L Whitfield, J Walker, W Jackson, R Woodward

Sitting: W D Megginson, W Wilson, J S Chubb (Captain), Rev J L Davies, E J Scott

Umpires: T B Topham and C Stead

Herbert Marshall & Dick Robinson of Sledmere Grange drilling

(Photo courtesy of Sheila Robinson)

School Photo outside the Village Hall in the 1940s.

Back row: Ivy Pudsey, Ruth Pudsey, Margaret Bowes, Doreen Kellington, ?, Dorothy Whitfield, ?, Angela Sygrove, Julia Stubbings, Daphne Stubbings, Barbara Holmes, Mike Owbridge, Chris Bowes, Martin Hardy, ?

2nd row: Clive Baker, Robbie Spence, Edward Bowes, Richard Hardy, Michael Scott, Brian Kent, Kenny Magee, Richard Sygrove, Billy Pudsey, Sam Sygrove, Keith Sinton, Derrick Kent, ?, Cyril Kellington

3rd row (beginning with children in front of pillar): Terry Walker, Brian Midgley, Clive Bowes, Eileen Midgley, Joe Metters, Jim Baker, Pam Jackson, Peggy Scott, Barbara Jackson, Shirley Jackson, Rosalie Scott, Beryl Sygrove, Edith Baker, Mary Sygrove, Doreen Kent,

4th row (seated): Gwen Southwick, Eileen Hornsea (now Conner), Heather Nicholson, Ernest Marshall, Christine Owbridge, Dorothy Robson, Mlle Ludovicy, Doug Robinson, Miss Cawood, ?, Pauline Sygrove, Ann Sygrove, Steve Stubbings, Dave Southwick

Front row: Christine Sygrove, ?, Helen Salter, Angela Marshall, Allen Pudsey, ?, Trevor Sinton, Ian Robinson, Rene Kent, John Lunn, ?, Malcolm Sygrove, ?

Dialect

By Chris Whitfield

Starting out at Secondary School in 1949 I was introduced to Latin, and told by both my English teacher and Latin teacher that this ancient language was introduced to this country by the Romans 2,000 years or so ago and was indeed the main foundation upon which the English language was based. On the other hand, both I and other boys from the High Wold villages were ridiculed for our broad East Yorkshire dialects. Consider our considerable delight, when at our customary Christmas Feast the after-dinner speaker was Mr Austin Hyde (then headmaster of Lady Lumley's Grammar School, Pickering) who told us many amusing stories and recited some of his poems in the East Yorkshire dialect. Vindication indeed!

We are told that the Saxons arrived in this country in AD 451 just over a hundred years after the Romans had departed these shores. In 545 Ida, a Saxon landed at Flamborough Head and subdued the Country from the Humber to the Forth and founded the kingdom of Northumbria. In 685, the Britons, totally subdued by the Saxons, retreated into Wales and Cornwall. In 787, the Danes first landed in Britain. In 832, they again invaded the Country, but were expelled and afterwards returned and ravaged the Kingdom. For a long time, unmolested, another invasion took place in 867. During these successive invasions, many a Norse boat, manned by sea warriors, and controlled by a Viking, landed on Flamborough Head, from where they spread themselves across the Wolds. The Danes were finally defeated in 880 by Alfred the Great who allowed them to settle in Northumbria if they agreed to embrace Christianity.

One of the great characters of our High Wold villages, the Reverend Edward Maule Cole, MA was vicar at Wetwang from 1865 – 1911 and is buried in the churchyard at Wetwang. In 1879 he published a pamphlet on Scandinavian place names. He showed how many of our village names were of Norse origin; Wetwang for example was Vettvangr. The former part of the word Vettr was a witness and the Vang was early Danish for a field – a place where Court was held and matters of the law settled.

Reference is also made to Sledmere, Fimber and Fridaythorpe. Interestingly locals still refer to the latter as "Fra-thrup", hundreds of years after the Danes were here. And the Danish word for Thorpe is "Thrup". The Rev Cole also points out that many surnames and also farms are of Scandinavian origin. He also includes a list of words used in East Yorkshire dialect and lists the Scandinavian words from which they were derived.

MOSES SOWERSBY.

One of the earlier poets to write in East Riding dialect was Moses Sowersby. Born at Wetwang in 1846 he lost his sight by accident in 1858 and in 1859, he entered the Yorkshire School for the Blind in York through the kind efforts of Miss Sykes, sister of Sir Tatton Sykes. He commenced writing poems in his teenage years. His poem "The Old Farmer's Tale" gives glimpses of what farming was like 100-150 years ago.

Walter Turner was vicar of Fridaythorpe from 1908 – 1917. He produced a collection of 23 short stories in prose called "Goodies". The first story, from which the book takes its name, is about a lady member of the congregation eating sweets in church. Many of the stories in "Goodies" give a lovely insight into life in these villages over 100 years ago.

Walter Turner also wrote poems and his poem "The Wolds Waggoner" tells us of the men of the Waggoners Reserve going to war in the 1914-1918 World War. He is seen here with his wife Emily and daughters Mary and Nancy.

George Hardwick was a grocer from Bridlington, and in the early 1900s wrote many poems and also stories in prose.

One of his poems was called "Lahtle Wetwang" and was written about the time of the First World War, and from this we get a picture of life on the farms in the early 1900s. At the back of his book, "Stories in Dialect", we have a long list of dialect words in the first column, the Scandinavian word from which they are derived in the second column, and the Standard English word in the third column.

The afore-mentioned Mr F Austin Hyde spent most of his life in the East and North Ridings of Yorkshire. His two most well known poems were "A Yorkshire Shepherd to his dog" and "Depper Auld Mare". The former was a tribute to the worth of a good sheepdog to the wold shepherd with large flocks of sheep, and the second poem tells of how the farm lads thought the world of the cart horses or shire horses they spent their working lives with. Here again a picture in words of the early 1900s. Mr Hyde also wrote many short and humorous sketches which were ideal for entertainment by the Women's Institute or churches of the day. His knowledge of the dialect and amusing stories meant he was much in demand as an entertainer and after dinner speaker. Highly educated people who looked down on the folk of the East Riding and their dialect really irritated him. He used to tell the story of a southerner in a flashy car who stopped and asked a local the way to Driffield. As the southerner had neglected to say please, the local gentleman said "Ah deean't know". The gentleman asked again if the local knew the way to Malton and once again neglected to say please, the local again said "Ah deean't know". The southerner said, "You don't know much, do you?" "Mebbe nut" said the local, "But ah isn't lost." Mr Hyde's sister, Muriel Carr, also wrote poems and "On a Farm" and "Frustration" are well worth reading.

Arthur Jarrett, like Austin Hyde was a Methodist local preacher and had offices in the Land of Green Ginger at the bottom of Whitefriargate in Hull. Arthur's poem "Sunday Skeeal Annivossary" paints a lovely and amusing picture of that special day in the Methodist calendar, and also "Lang Sermons", "Harvest Festival", "Keesmas Singing", and "The Innkeeper". Arthur used to tell the story of a large Australian sheep farmer who came to the East Riding for a holiday. He got into conversation with a local farmer and asked how big his holding was. "Well !" said the farmer, "I starts aback o' yon wood, gans roond bi that thorn hedge, an' back ti t'rooad along yan wire fence. It's a fairish size". "Good heavens" said the Australian, "Listen to this! A month ago I went round my farm. I went by car. Believe it or not, it took me two and a half days!" "Ah knaw" said the farmer. "Ah'd a car like that but ah seean gat shut on it".

Geoff Robinson was also a Methodist local preacher. In his early days he lived at Garton on the Wolds and worked for E B Bradshaw and Sons at Bell Mills, Driffield. Of all the writers of East Riding dialect Geoff was the most prolific. He started writing his poems at an early age and for many years wrote a weekly poem in the Hull and East Yorkshire Times under the pen name of "Old Joss". He produced two books of poems and prose. As a tribute to him after his death, the East Riding Dialect Society collected together what they considered his best poems, which they recently published.

For keeping dialect in the public eye, the dialect societies play a prominent part. The Yorkshire Dialect Society, founded in 1897 has over a thousand members, some of which are in the East Riding and some in the High Wolds Heritage Group. The Yorkshire Dialect Society covers a vast area from Middlesbrough in the north, south to Spurn Point, west to the independent republic of Saddleworth, north again to Sedbergh and south to Sheffield. The dialects vary greatly but we who are members can generally understand each other. The society has many publications, books, tapes and CDs. Each year it produces two books; "Summer Bulletin" which is mainly a collection of poems and prose written by members and "Transactions of the Yorkshire Dialect Society" which includes information, accounts, history of dialect and a wide range of topics relating to dialect. Some of our local East Riding writers and dialect speakers feature including Jack Danby, Irwin Bielby and a reprint of "Goodies" by Walter Turner with illustrations by Jack Danby. The Society generally has two meetings each year which are open to all members.

Much nearer to home is the East Riding Dialect Society begun in 1984 by Audrey Bemrose and her husband Don. This society has about 100 members and produces 3 or 4 newsletters each year. Members are encouraged to write dialect poems and prose for the newsletters and over recent years have produced books of poems or prose in East Riding dialect. George Nellist, from Sledmere who was a reader in the Church of England wrote "The Yorkshire Wolds of Yesteryear", Ron Wray's collection of poems was entitled "Rural Ramblings", Eric Lount's book was "The Writing's On The Wall", founder of the society, Don Bemrose wrote "Diz Thoo Remember" and Phil Copeland "Bits of this and that". Along with Geoff Robinson's books, "Humour from the Ridings" and "Yorkshire Smiles", the society also has CDs and a very comprehensive dictionary of East Riding dialect words produced by the late Norman Stockton. The society generally has six meetings each year as well as a "Yorkshire Day" at Pocklington, usually on the first Saturday in August. This event consists of entertainment by members of the East Riding Dialect Society with a Yorkshire Tea half way through. In addition to the meetings there is a Mell Supper and a Charter Dinner. We Yorkshire folk like our food!

Our High Wolds Heritage Group has fostered the use of dialect by having speakers on East Riding dialect from within our group and beyond.

Ivy Eden and Chris Whitfield,
members of the
High Wolds Heritage Group,
presenting dialect poems and stories.

A booklet "Words on the Wolds" has been produced by the group. This contains poems and prose, some in the dialect of the East Riding of Yorkshire, about the people, villages and countryside of the Yorkshire Wolds. There are contributions from residents, and former residents of the High Wold Villages. The main writer is Ivy Eden, who has brought so much fun and good humour by entertaining in the East Riding dialect. Other writers, previously mentioned in this article, also have contributions.

Much of our dialect is steeped in history both recent and not so recent and we can tend to look at the past through rose coloured spectacles, but Walter Turner makes us stop and think with his poem "The Good Awd Tahmes". A farm labourer's wages were poor, work was hard and long, and food was very basic. The following are the first four verses of Walter Turner's poem which attempts to put the record straight.

"The good awd tahmes? The good awd tahmes?
An yer think at yer 'd like 'em back? Then Ah'll tell yer what, by Gaw!
You just should a lived as a lad when Ah did, an then yer'd knaw
Better 'an ax for t' good awd tahmes.

They're better awaah is t' good awd tahmes,
Wi their opper an gallusies, lays, an flaals, it was ard dree wark;
Gerrin up i' t' morn afoor leet, an laabourin wharl lang efter dark!
Deean't tell me aboot t' good awd tahmes.

Me faather ee threshed, i' t' good awd tahmes
At Towthrop, a fower mahle walk, an mebbe be there afore fahve.
An ee yance get yam afoor seven at neet, ee'd getten a drahve,
A rare thing that, i' t' good awd tahmes.

An what could ee addle, i' t' good awd tahmes?
Ah'll tell yer; ee addled eight shillin a week, an they gav im his meeat,
San wi six growin bairns at yam, you may bet there was monny a treeat
Oot o' that for us, i' t' good awd tahmes."

I like the description of the East Riding dialect taken from Mr Morris's "East Yorkshire Folk Speech". He writes, *"these lonesome spots, these distant valleys and hills, these isolated cottages and farms, these homely firesides, wherever, in short, the rich and racy language of the old Yorkshire folk is spoken in its time-honoured purity and fullness, I look upon as almost sacred places. For in spite of its seeming ruggedness, there is an unspeakable tenderness about it, which those who are born to it only know, and can never resist. It is, after all in many thousands of cases, even still, the true language of the heart. For ages and generations it has been the vehicle for conveying between people who have in their veins the best blood of the Anglo-Saxon race, all their deepest thoughts, as well as their noblest and tenderest feelings. Its familiar tones and cadences have been heard through many long centuries, in times of joy and happiness, as well as in days of darkness and sorrow. They have sealed the steadfastness of true lovers; they have lent music to the innocent prattle of children's voices; they have carried a mother's welcome to the soldier or sailor lad returned safe and sound from the din of the battlefield or the perils of the deep, to the threshold of his home once more"*.

May the homely dialect of our East Riding folk still be heard in our villages and market towns for years to come!!

Thixendale

An aerial view of Thixendale village which gives a clear idea of the layout. New buildings can be seen at both ends of the village. Beamer Hill, on the right, looks delightful in the spring when the May blossom is out.

This photograph was taken in 1921 by the Rev WA Schofield, who was a keen photographer until he lost his sight. Beamer view cottages, built in 1907, are on the left and the beck can be seen on the right.

This view of the village in the 1950s shows bungalows and semi-detached houses built by the council. The chalk cottages further up the street, shown in the previous photograph, had been demolished by this time.

Thixendale in the snow – March 1985. This view of the centre of the village, taken from Beamer Hill, shows the village hall, the original Hillfoot Cottage, and Manor Farm in the distance.

The elm tree. Local residents referred to this as the 'Ome' tree; the name could possibly be derived from Norman French – orme – elm. The tree was felled in the 1970s.

An aerial view taken in the 1960s, focussing on the school, school house and garden, which was cultivated by the school children. Large gardens can be seen behind Diamond Cottages and the outbuilding behind the carrier's cottage would originally have been used for stable and cart shed. The petrol pump on the right, in front of Church View, was installed by Ken Coates, the blacksmith.

The vicarage, church and school, all designed by GE Street, the eminent Victorian architect, were built between 1868 – 1876. The earthwork enclosures of the original village layout can be seen behind the buildings.

St Mary's Church in July 1922. Little has changed to this external view of the church. The yew trees have grown and there is now a footpath and surfaced road.

Interior view from the altar of St Mary's Church – 2009. The bust of Sir Tatton Sykes, 5th Baronet and patron of the church, is on the chancel windowsill. The richly decorated organ pipes can be seen on the left.

The Cross Keys pub and 'Round the Bend' in 1967. The small building between them was a wash house. 'Round the Bend' is now one of the oldest inhabited houses in the village.

This sketch of Hillfoot Cottage by Nicholson, dated 12th July 1810, is the earliest picture of Thixendale known by the authors. The road to Malton is gated and the cottage is thatched, as were other chalk cottages in the village.

Hillfoot Cottage in 1923. The group of men with the horses are at the pond. The tree, which gave its name to Ash Tree Farm, died and was felled.

Working horses at the village pond – possibly early 1920s. The men are sitting side saddle.

Robert and Jimmy Boyes with Jack Midgley. The horses are pulling a Cambridge roller.

The Headmistress of the school, Miss Whitehead, took this photograph in 1922. The flue protruding from the roof (not visible on earlier photographs) shows that a stove had been put into the schoolroom. All the original doorways into the school were preserved when the building was restored in 2004.

The village children in fancy dress to celebrate the coronation of King George VI in 1937.

Mrs Benson with her class in 1950. She was a highly respected headteacher, artistic and musical. She was joint founder of Thixendale WI with Mrs Jeannie Bell of Burdale.

Back row: Doreen Morley, Raymond Suggitt, Dorothy Walker, Harry Boyes, Ivy Jefferson, Brian Hill, Patricia Cooper, Andrew Cooper, Marjorie Sherburn, Mrs Benson.

Front row: John Brayshaw, Susan Fletcher, Joan Walker, Pauline Hill, Marion Cooper, Francis Strangeway, Anthony Brayshaw.

Thixendale WI trip to Blackpool in 1955.

Left to Right: Marjorie Owston, Ruth Hill, Doreen Morley, Anne Boyes, Mrs Hepton, Jeannie Bell, Amy Bell, Evelyn Brent, Mrs Sercombe, Maude Jefferson, Ida Sercombe.

Having responsibility for the maintenance of the grade 2 listed church and village hall has led to the community finding innovative ways of raising funds. Events have included the Highway Robbery (1991), Great Yorkshire Pudding Event (1989), and one of the first scarecrow festivals (1989)

Left to right: Lelania Atkinson, Pauline Foster, Keith Bristow, Maude Smith, Madge Jefferson, Emma Brader on Pepper, Anne Thornton, Charlotte Brader on Falcon.

In front: Otto Hughes and Shelly Hepton.

Wetwang

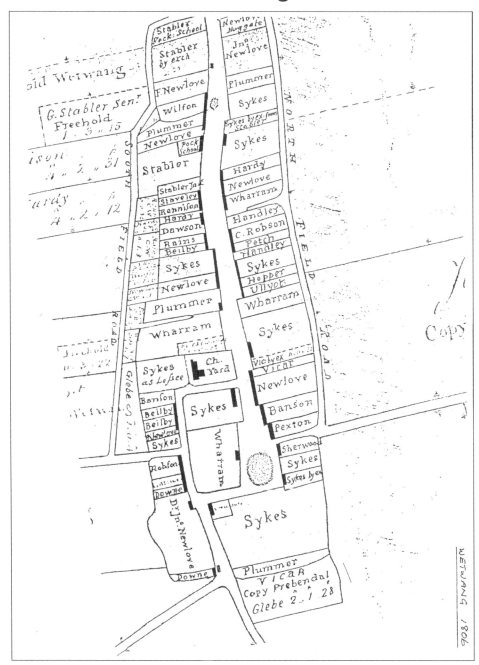

The 1806 map of Wetwang shows who owned each portion of land at the time of enclosure. The houses (indicated in black) were relatively few in number.

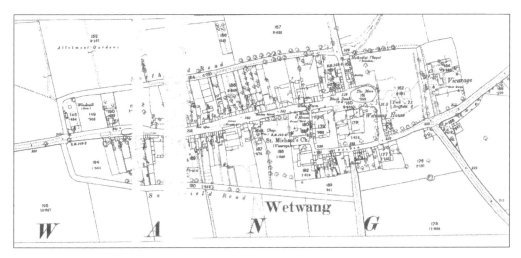

Eighty years later in 1886 many changes have taken place. The 1801 Census shows a population of 193 and by 1881 it had trebled to 623. In the ensuing years the railway had come, the school had been built in 1843, chapels in 1812 and 1824 and a vicarage at the east end of the village.

A happy group of Sunday School children from Wetwang St. Nicholas' Church, 1934, with Vicar Rev. Hammond standing behind.

Left to right back row: Annie Thurlow, Jean Waites, Mavis Rowley, Rebecca Sims, Sheila Hotham, Elsie Thurlow.

Middle row: Reg Sims, Jimmy Brown, Sam Serginson, Not Known, Geoff Wilson.

Front row: Bobby Botterill, Fred Coldham.

The Primitive Methodist Chapel was built in 1824 then rebuilt in 1869. This was situated at the top of Station Hill and entry was by two doors at the front. The pulpit was at the front between the doors and after a small communion/ choir area the pews sloped steeply upwards to the back of the chapel. Entry to the schoolroom and other ancillary rooms was from the chapel or by a path to the left of the chapel.

The Wesleyan Methodist Chapel was built in 1886, whilst the original chapel of 1812 continued as a Sunday school. Today the chapel of 1812 is the village shop. The chapel of 1886 (pictured here) had decorative grey-white bricks for a frontage and ordinary bricks in the rest of the building. Note the wrought ironwork, which was sawn off in the 2nd World War, as there was a shortage of iron for armaments etc. This chapel was closed in 1964 and demolished in 1978.

A photograph of some of the Wetwang schoolchildren in 1893. The Headmaster on the right is Mr Parsons and the master on the left is thought to be Mr William Myers.

Harvesting at Holmfield Farm in the late 1940s or early 1950s. The man on the right of the two forking the sheaves is thought to be Mr Boswell (Farm Foreman) and the man on top of the load is Charlie Cooper. Note the wooden frames to stack the sheaves against called "gormers".

One of the earliest combine harvesters, possibly in the 1960s. This would have a 10 or 12-foot wide cut and maybe harvest 10 to 12 acres a day. Some of the largest combines today have a 40-foot wide cut, harvesting 150-170 acres per day. Pictured driving the combine is Alec Serginson, driving the Fordson tractor is George Culley and admiring their handiwork is Farmer Jeff Beal of Woods Farm.

In the yard of T. Dale and Sons butcher's shop. Left to right: Mr Tom Dale, with daughter Marjorie, Wills Serginson and Charlie Yarker. The bullock with great conformation is a Shorthorn, most probably red and white or possibly blue and white.

The names of the carriers of Wetwang can be found in old directories. In the early days they attended Driffield markets taking produce and people, with horses doing the transporting. Later motorised vehicles took over and Len ("Panch") Broadley set up in business. His exploits are recorded in a little book entitled "Keeping off the Dole".

Mr Swinn with the three-wheeled bicycle cum cart, which it is said, he made himself. Note the cart on the left with a wheel missing and the rulley (a flat four wheeled wagon used for conveyance of goods) in the background.

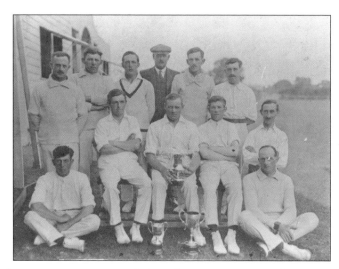

Wetwang had many very successful cricket teams over the years. This team of the 1920s won the Driffield Evening Cup on three occasions in that decade. The "Driffield Evening Cup" was the blue ribbon competition in the East Riding.

Back row: Len Hardy, John Danby, G S Wilson, Dewsbury Megginson, Charlie Whitfield, George Huggins

Middle row: Charlie Barnes, John Megginson, Eric Swinn, Harry Hodge

Front row, seated: Fred Wilson, P C Townsend

Possibly Wetwang's most successful football team, photographed in the season after the end of World War 2. Note the five cups won by the team in that year.

Back row: G Main, J Kilvington, A Swaby, H Cooper, R Hodgson, R Simms

Middle row: S Sissons, F Oxtoby, E Blowman, J Owen (Capt), F Simpson, S Lowe, S Cook

Front row, seated: D Hodgson, F Wilson

Each year the Hull and East Riding Institute for the Blind held a sale in Wetwang of produce made by their members. Tickets were sold weekly in the village and on the day of the sale were used to buy the various items. Pictured outside the old Village Hall on a snowy day, proudly showing off their purchases, are Paul Pattinson, Linda Gladwell and Ian Main.

Pictured at a sumptuous Wetwang Women's Institute Dinner, obviously enjoying themselves are:

Standing left to right: Ann Wilson, Shirley Parker, Cora Waite, Mary Newlove, Mrs Mears and Mary Ann Lunn.

Seated: Ethel Brown, Freda Newby, Elsie Gascoyne, Nancy Sawdon, Lena Young, Shirley Brocklesby and Elsie Lomax.

Wetwang Fire Brigade of the 1950s in front of their fire engine with the inscription "No 14 Station".

Left to right: Syd Cook, John Coldham, Bill Mason, Curly Hancil, Reg Hodgson and Albert Swaby.

The Fire Station in the background is now Harper's Fish and Chip Shop with the title "The Old Fire Plaice".

Wetwang post mill at the western end of the village. The miller turned the top portion of the mill to make use of the wind direction. Note the miller's house on the right, which was built with one floor below ground level so that the house didn't get in the way of a southerly wind!

In the 1920s and 1930s a village fair was held each year in Wetwang to raise funds for a village hall. Pictured above is a procession of floats led by a band in Main Street. Inset, the village street today.

This happy photo of Richard Whiteley chatting to Jane Craig (nee Foster) is at a school fair in the 1990s. Richard was known to make fun of Wetwang on his Countdown programme, so Jane (of the Wetwang Parent Teachers' Association) asked Richard to open the school fete and he agreed. He was made "Mayor of Wetwang" and also attended the very successful "Scarecrow Festivals".

Over the years Wetwang has produced many famous sons and daughters. Perhaps the most famous was Sir John Huggins KCMG who became Governor of Jamaica. Sir John was the son of a Wetwang bricklayer and went to school in Wetwang, Driffield and Bridlington. In the above photo he and his family are pictured arriving in Jamaica in December 1943.

Many of Wetwang's early houses were built of chalk. This photograph round about 1900 shows the bottom pond before it was enclosed. Also two rows of chalk houses called "Teapot Row", with a shop on the corner. These houses were demolished in the 1930s. Inset, the same view today.